COLLEGE INSTRUCTOR'S HANDBOOK

by

Lisa Savy Kauffman

ISBN-13 # 979-8-218-58576-1

TABLE OF CONTENTS

FOREWORD

Congratulations! You have either accepted a position as a college instructor, or are in the process of applying. If you are in the latter category, you will want to start with Appendix A: Getting Hired.

You may already be established in your position as a college instructor. In that case, you may want to skip the section on Onboarding and jump directly to the sections that interest you.

As you embark on your journey as a new (or established) instructor, I hope that you find this handbook a comprehensive guide designed to support you in navigating the multifaceted world of college teaching.

Higher education is a transformative endeavor, both for students and for those who have chosen the noble profession of teaching. You will want your classroom (in person or virtual) to be a place where minds are molded, critical thinking is honed, and lifelong learning is fostered. The role you play as an instructor is pivotal in this process, serving not just as a conveyor of knowledge but as a mentor, a guide, and an inspiration to your students.

This handbook has been crafted to serve as your companion throughout this rewarding yet challenging journey. Within these pages, you will find insights into the principles of effective pedagogy and practical advice on the myriad aspects of academic life. From course design and assessment methods to fostering academic integrity and integrating technology into your teaching, each chapter is designed to equip you with the tools and knowledge necessary for success in the classroom.

In addition to pedagogical guidance, this handbook also addresses institutional policies, grading practices, student support services, and professionalism.

As you explore this handbook, I encourage you to adapt its recommendations to your unique teaching style and the specific needs of your students. Teaching is both an art and a science, and there is no one-size-fits-all approach. Your creativity, empathy, and dedication will be your greatest assets as you navigate your teaching career.

I also urge you to view this handbook not as a static document but as a starting point for ongoing dialogue and collaboration. Engage with your colleagues, seek out mentorship, and participate in the professional learning communities within your institution. The exchange of ideas and experiences is invaluable in fostering innovation and excellence in teaching.

Finally, remember that the impact you have on your students extends beyond the classroom. Your enthusiasm, commitment, and support can ignite a passion for learning that resonates throughout their lives. As educators, we have the privilege and responsibility to shape the future, one student at a time.

1: THE NEW HIRE

College Onboarding

You've received that exhilarating, potentially life-changing phone call – you're hired! Whether as a full-time tenure track, temporary contract, or adjunct instructor, there are important first steps to navigate. First, a few terms:

College – The Institution of Higher Learning at which you will be employed, whether public or private. It could actually be a university, but for brevity we'll go with the word *college*. (A **university** can be thought of as a college superset: it offers a broader range of undergraduate degrees as well as graduate degrees.)

School – A division of the college comprised of more than one department; for example *School of Mathematics & Science*.

Department – A specific subject area, such as *Mathematics*. Usually, each department conducts its own applicant search and hiring, through the college.

CHAPTER 1

Semester – the length of a course. Colleges usually have 16-week semesters (two per year) or 10-week quarters (three per year), not including a Summer session. I will use the term *semester* interchangeably with the term *quarter*.

The initial phone call (hopefully it was a phone call rather than email) probably came from someone in the department or school. This phone call hopefully gave you pertinent information about **onboarding**.

Typically your first onboarding experience will take place at the college level and will be organized by the Human Resources department. This is usually a week or two before the semester starts. They will require you to submit **official transcripts** from every institution you've attended. Get started on this as quickly as possible. Find out, from Human Resources, how the transcripts will be transmitted.

Human Resources will then send you an **employment contract** which includes your pay grade and amount. For full-time instructors, your initial salary will depend on your highest education level and previous teaching experience. For part-time, your pay will probably depend on the number of units you will be teaching. The Human Resources section of the college's website will probably include a pay scale. I have included a sample pay scale in Appendix B.

You will be required to attend an orientation with Human Resources in which they explain the benefits available to you. You will sign forms such as the IRS **W-4 form** (income tax deductions) and the DHS **I-9 form** (Employment Eligibility Verification). The latter will require some combination of ID cards/documents to prove your identity. This form can be found at i-9.pdf (uscis.gov). Look over the options and make sure you are prepared to provide the necessary information. Some of the documents may need to be originals, such as a social security card.

You may be required to pass a drug test, TB test, and/or provide proof of vaccination(s). You may need to agree to a **criminal background check** and/or obtain **fingerprints**.

This is also a good time to ask about a **parking permit** and **photo ID badge**, if required. The college undoubtedly provides **wi-fi access** – is there a secure wi-fi connection available exclusively to instructors? What is the password?

You will be given a username and password to the college's **Human Resources web portal**, such as workday.com. Hopefully the college allows you to use the same username/password to access *all* its online services and interfaces, which should include:

- **Email**
- **Phone number**
- **Technology Services** (for tech support)
- **Inservice Registration for Instructors**
- **Student Registration Portal** (such as PeopleSoft)
- **Student Learning Portal** (such as Canvas and Blackboard)

Department Items

The following items should be provided by your school or department:

- **Key** to your office/workspace
- A **computer** (If it is a laptop, are you able to take it home?)
- Access to a **printer**
- Access to a **xerox** machine (does it require a code? Do you have a limit?)
- Location of your **mailbox**
- Your **teaching schedule** (more about this in the next chapter: **Getting Ready for the First Day**)
- How to **access the classroom(s)** you will be using ... master key card? Access code?
- Name/location/contact info of **Department Administrative Assistant**

Some colleges have **printing departments** which can help with large photocopy jobs. Will your department prefer you to submit large orders to the printing department, for example final exams?

The Department Administrative Assistant will be one of, if not THE, most important campus contact for you. This person can help you with office and classroom supplies such as **dry erase markers**. (You can never have enough dry erase markers. Don't ever leave them behind in the classroom or you'll never see them again. Or you'll come back and they'll be all dried out. Take them with you!)

> *The Department Administrative Assistant is the go-to person for questions you are too embarrassed to ask anyone else.*

Or ... you may be assigned a **mentor** in your department. This person should share with you all the insider information you need to be successful. (Much like this handbook)

Inservice Training

At my college, we have what are called **Convocation Weeks** twice a year, each in the week prior to the start of classes. Keep in mind each college has their own agenda. I will share that of my own college, as a sample.

Do not plan a vacation during this week.

The week begins with a college-wide address in which the college president and other high ranking administrators deliver a welcome/motivational message. Achievement statistics are discussed, as well as goals, mission statements, etc.

The second day of Convocation Week is reserved for School and Department meetings. At these meetings the respective chairs will discuss relevant information to the school/department.

The remainder of Convocation Week is devoted to an offering of **professional development** trainings. There are often several to choose from in each time slot. They may be offered in person or online. These mini-courses include topics such as pedagogy, various software usage, available resources, student services, etc.

In your first semester, you will be given a list of **required training** for new employees. At my college, these trainings include:

- Sexual Harassment and Discrimination Prevention
- Diversity 101
- FEMA Active Shooter Training
- Building Supportive Communities: Clery Act and Title IX
- College Policy Against Unlawful Discrimination and Harassment

You will be told whether these need to be completed prior to the first day of classes, or whether they can be taken during the semester.

In summary, successful onboarding involves understanding institutional culture, navigating policies, utilizing resources, building networks, preparing for teaching, adapting to new responsibilities, and fostering continuous growth. By focusing on these areas, you create a strong foundation for your career as a college instructor, positioning yourself for success and fulfillment in your academic role.

2: SEMESTER PLAN

It is the supreme art of the teacher to awaken joy in creative expression and knowledge. — Albert Einstein

Teaching Schedule

You should have already received a copy of your **teaching schedule** which lists your courses and the days/times/modalities in which they will be taught. The **modality** is one of the following:

- In Person Classes
- Hybrid Classes – part online, part in person
- Online Classes with scheduled live lessons via web conferencing (synchronous)
- Online Classes with no scheduled live lessons (asynchronous)

If you are very lucky, you will have an opportunity to choose any or all of your schedule, although that is unlikely in your first semester. This is because schedules are arranged several months in advance, to allow students the opportunity to enroll.

Your schedule might even change in the first week. Low enrollment courses may be cancelled. You might be assigned a different course at the last minute, although a prudent department chair will avoid burdening new instructors with that responsibility.

A prudent department chair will also try to assign as few teaching **preps** as possible to new instructors. For example, if you are teaching three *Beginning Composition* courses, two *Advanced Composition* courses, and an *Intro to Shakespeare* course, that is considered three preps because you will be preparing three distinct lesson plans.

Textbooks

For each course that you will be teaching, you should be provided with some sort of **course description** which describes the objectives and recommended textbook/materials. Often this information can be found on your college's website. For your first semester, use the **recommended textbook/materials**. Most likely a committee chose that textbook based on extensive research. As you gain experience teaching the course, you may decide to eventually choose a different textbook (if allowed by your department). In the meantime, get a copy of your textbooks. They will probably be provided by the Department Administrative Assistant. You can also request teacher editions directly from the publisher. The major publishers (Pearson, McGraw-Hill etc.) have regional sales reps who can assist you with selecting and reviewing textbooks.

If you are in a position to select your own textbook, do not overlook **Open-Source** textbooks of which the online versions are free to students. A very good source is OpenStax.org.

For introductory courses, your department may also provide what is called a **course shell** in the **LMS** (**Learning Management System**). This would be a turnkey package with preprogrammed assignments, discussions, lessons etc. It will greatly ease your burden of lesson planning. (More about LMS's in Chapter 3.)

This brings us to the issue of **autonomy** in course design. Some departments, for some courses, may require you to follow a very rigid schedule in which you cover specific objectives each week from a specific textbook, with specific assignments, and require you to administer department-authored exams on specific days or weeks. I have found this often to be required by private universities geared toward working adults. These institutions of dubious accreditation rely almost exclusively on adjunct instructors with little or no experience, offering them little pay, and resulting in high instructor turnover.

On the plus side, these pre-packaged courses reduce individual lesson planning and ensure department uniformity. On the negative side, they do not allow you to allocate instructional time based on student mastery.

Conversely, some departments may thrust a new course at you with simply a broad course description and no resources/materials. Basically, you're on your own. I know of one new instructor who was told to design a *Crew Resource Management* course for the Aviation department. He was given only that – the title of the course. Fortunately this was the exception rather than the norm.

Online Learning Platforms

Many textbook publishers offer websites called **Online Learning Platforms** or **Educational Technology Platforms**. Essentially these websites deliver homework problems which students answer and submit to the platform. Many of them offer hints and videos. Some of them offer personalized learning (these are called **Adaptive Learning Platforms**). As an instructor, you have many options to set up the homework assignments and grading.

Math platforms include **MyMathLab** (Pearson), **WebAssign** (Cengage), **XYZhomework** (XYZ Textbooks), **ALEKS** (McGraw-Hill), **MyOpenLab** (free or low cost, very customizable, offers turnkey courses for many Open Source textbooks), and **Lumen OHM** (similar to MyOpenLab). However there are OLP's for virtually every subject, and more added every day.

These are amazing time-savers for instructors, and provide students with immediate feedback and the opportunity to re-do problems until mastery is achieved.

A concern, particularly for math and science, is that there are many problem-solving programs, apps and websites that will provide the answers. They even show the problem-solving steps.

Some of the OLP's give you (the instructor) the option to require students to scan and submit 'work' for the questions. Of course, you will now have to review every question in every homework for every student. Perhaps it's best to reserve that level of scrutiny for grading tests.

With your schedule, course materials, and course descriptions in hand, you are ready to prepare your Scope & Sequence and syllabi.

Scope & Sequence

Before you put together your syllabi, you need to have an idea of what you will cover and when. This is defined in the Scope & Sequence which may or may not be provided by your department.

The **Scope and Sequence** in lesson planning are crucial elements that guide the structure and delivery of educational content over a specified period. They ensure that instruction is coherent, comprehensive, and appropriately paced to achieve educational objectives. Here's an in-depth look at each component:

Scope

Scope refers to the breadth and depth of content covered in a course or subject area. It outlines what topics, concepts, and skills students will learn. The scope includes:

- **Content Coverage:** Specifies what will be taught (e.g., topics, themes, units).
- **Skills and Competencies:** Details the skills students will develop (e.g., critical thinking, problem-solving).
- **Learning Objectives:** Clarifies what students should know and be able to do by the end of the course or unit.
- **Instructional Goals:** Reflects overarching goals of the curriculum and individual lessons.
- **Alignment with Standards:** Ensures that the content aligns with national, state, or institutional standards and benchmarks.

Example: In a high school biology course, the scope might include major topics such as cellular biology, genetics, evolution, and ecology.

It also details the specific concepts within each topic, such as cell structure, genetic inheritance, natural selection, and ecosystem dynamics.

Sequence

Sequence refers to the order in which the content and skills are taught. It organizes the learning progression to ensure logical development and build on prior knowledge. The sequence involves:

- **Order of Instruction:** Establishes a logical flow of topics, from simple to complex, or from foundational to advanced.
- **Pacing:** Determines the amount of time allocated to each topic, ensuring sufficient depth and understanding.
- **Prerequisite Knowledge:** Identifies prior knowledge required before introducing new topics.
- **Integration:** Shows how different topics or units interconnect and support overall understanding.
- **Scaffolding:** Provides instructional support structures that gradually diminish as students gain mastery.

Example: In a math course, the sequence might start with basic arithmetic, followed by introduction to algebraic concepts, then progress to more complex topics like functions and equations. Each topic builds on the previous one, ensuring students have the necessary foundation for understanding more advanced material.

Scope and Sequence: Working Together

When combined, the scope and sequence provide a clear roadmap for educators to design their lessons effectively. Here's how they complement each other:

- **Curriculum Design:** Teachers use the scope to identify what content and skills are essential and then plan the sequence to arrange these elements in a meaningful order.
- **Lesson Planning:** Helps in breaking down the course into manageable units or modules, each with specific learning objectives aligned with the overall scope.

- **Instructional Strategies:** Guides the choice of teaching methods, ensuring that they are appropriate for the content and sequential development.
- **Assessment:** Assists in planning formative and summative assessments that align with the scope (what is being assessed) and sequence (when it is being assessed).

By thoughtfully planning the scope and sequence, educators create a structured yet flexible framework that supports effective teaching and enhances student learning outcomes.

A sample Scope & Sequence is included in Appendix C.

Syllabus

You only have one chance to make a first impression.

The syllabus is a cornerstone of effective teaching and learning in a college setting. It serves as a comprehensive guide and contract between the instructor and students, clearly outlining course objectives, expectations, assessment methods, and key policies. By providing a detailed roadmap of the course, the syllabus helps students understand the scope of the material, deadlines, and grading criteria, fostering a sense of responsibility and time management. It also sets the tone for the course, reflecting the instructor's academic standards and pedagogical approach. Moreover, the syllabus is an essential tool for ensuring academic integrity and consistency, serving as a reference for dispute resolution and as a framework for accreditation and curriculum development. In essence, a well-crafted syllabus enhances transparency, promotes engagement, and supports the overall academic success of students.

You will first want to find out if the college and/or department has a boilerplate syllabus format. Or they may have "plug-in paragraphs" to describe the college's various policies on Academic Integrity, Counseling and Tutoring Resources, etc. More about the various components of a syllabus below.

I also recommend you get one or more recent **syllabi** from your department colleagues for each course you will be teaching. (My college has a department drive in which all instructors must upload their syllabi and final exams.) Compare and contrast the various elements such as grading schema. In your first year of teaching, you do not want to deviate too far from the norm when structuring your own courses.

A good college course syllabus is comprehensive and well-organized, providing a clear framework for the course. A sample syllabus (my own) is in Appendix D. Essential components include:

Course Information

Title and Section: Full name of the course, section number, and modality. If synchronous, include the days/times. If in person, include the location.

Term and Year: Semester or term along with the academic year.

Instructor Details: Name, office location, contact information, office hours, preferred method of communication, and preferred pronouns if you wish. If you have a professional web page, include that. Do NOT include any social media; in fact immediately set your privacy settings on social media to 'private' not 'public.'

Course Description

Catalog Description: A one-paragraph overview from the course catalog.

Objectives and Learning Outcomes: Clear goals outlining what students are expected to learn and be able to do by the end of the course.

Prerequisites: Any prior knowledge or courses needed.

Course Materials

Required Texts and Resources: Textbooks, articles, software, or other materials. As previously mentioned, make sure you check with your department for any required or recommended textbooks.

Supplementary Materials: Additional readings or resources that support the course content.

Technology Requirements: Hardware and software needed, including any specific platforms or tools, calculators etc. If the course has a synchronous online component, then include details about the video conferencing software: Zoom, Microsoft Teams, Google Meet, etc. If you plan to record the online meetings, will you make them available on the LMS?

Course Schedule

Weekly Topics: A detailed schedule of topics, readings, and assignments by week or class session.

Important Dates: Dates for exams, major assignments, and holidays or breaks.

Assessment and Grading

Evaluation Methods: Description of how students will be assessed (exams, quizzes, projects, participation, portfolios, etc).

Grading Scale: Breakdown of the grading system (percentage or point-based) and weight of each component.

Assignment Submission: Guidelines for submitting assignments, including deadlines and late policies.

Test Administration: If your course is web-based, how will your tests be administered? With the proliferation of web-based courses, exam integrity is becoming a big issue. Is there a testing center that is available to proctor your in-person tests? Chances are they are not equipped for that volume of test proctoring. (The testing centers at my college are available for make-up tests only.) Will you be proctoring your own tests, and if so, is it necessary for you to reserve a classroom in advance?

Alternately, you may decide to implement an online proctored test service such as **ProctorU** and **Respondus**. These utilities may already be included in your college's LMS. Typically, these utilities require the student to take the exam alone (so a college computer lab would be unacceptable) and have a built-in camera. A remote human proctor will require the student to hold up a photo ID; the student will then be monitored via the camera throughout the exam (continuously or intermittently).

Regardless of whether you choose to use in-person proctoring or online proctoring, students will need to know this at the onset of the semester (preferably before). At my college, any requirement for in-person testing is included in the online college catalog so students are aware before they even sign up for the course.

Because Assessment and Grading is the foundation of your course, it will be discussed more thoroughly in the next section.

Course Policies

Attendance and Participation: Expectations for class attendance and participation.

Late Work and Make-up Policy: Rules for late submissions and make-up assignments or exams.

Academic Integrity: Policies on cheating, plagiarism, and collaboration. You will want to specifically address the usage of AI/ChatGPT – how much, if any, is acceptable? In mathematics courses, there is a plethora of apps and websites that will solve math problems. This is a constantly evolving issue, and popular department meeting discussion topic, as students become more sophisticated in using these tools to do their homework. Be proactive by spelling out what is and is not considered a breach of academic integrity. Also include possible consequences, at both the course and college level.

Classroom Etiquette: Expectations for behavior in class and online. While college level classrooms are inordinately more well-behaved than high school classrooms, you may need to set boundaries and guidelines especially regarding how to respectfully communicate with classmates and yourself. Be clear about **cell phone usage**. These devices should be on mute/vibrate and out of sight. It is understandable that adult college students have families, possibly jobs, and other responsibilities requiring contact by mobile phone. Instruct students to quietly remove themselves from the classroom to take critical calls.

Student Support

Accessibility Services: Information on how to access disability support and accommodations.

Academic Support: Resources like tutoring centers, libraries, or writing centers. Make sure students are aware of computer labs and wi-fi access.

Health and Wellness: Contact information for counseling and health services.

Financial Assistance: In addition to traditional financial aid, your college may offer some kind of emergency fund for disadvantaged students to help them purchase items like textbooks and supplies.

Communication Guidelines

Instructor Communication: Preferred methods and times for contact. Include office hours; the minimum number of hours will be specified by your department. Do not give out your cell phone number – students can reach you through your office phone number. The campus phone system will no doubt have a message system that will email you audio files of messages left on your office phone. Do not use or give out your personal email address.

If your college's LMS includes a messaging system, go to the settings and have it forward messages to your college email address. That way you only need to monitor one mailbox for incoming messages.

Class Communication: How announcements will be made (e.g., via email, course management system).

Emergency Information

Safety Procedures: Instructions on what to do in case of emergencies.

Campus Resources: Contact details for campus security and emergency services. If the campus has an app for emergency announcements, encourage students to download the app.

Additional Information

Supplementary Policies: Any additional course-specific policies or guidelines.

Changes to the Syllabus: Statement on how and when the syllabus may be revised.

If you skipped through any part of the above syllabus discussion, you can assume your students will also. It is recommended that you assign some sort of **Syllabus Quiz/Acknowledgement** the first week of the course. For my own courses, I create a multiple-choice quiz on the Canvas LMS with questions about the grading schema, late homework policy, make-up test policy, etc. ... i.e. the most common topics that students email me about because they did not read the syllabus.

If you are teaching an in person course, you can choose to print out copies of the syllabi and hand them out in class. However the push for a paperless classroom should start here. Upload a pdf copy of the syllabus to the college's LMS, or an easy place for students to find it. On the first day of the course, show the students how to navigate to the syllabus, and highlight the key points. Do not read it to them word-for-word: they know how to read and you'll be wasting time. Hopefully your classroom will have a screen/projector which you can use to project content from a computer or tablet device.

Lastly, does your college and/or department require you to submit copies of your syllabi? Make sure you do that.

The Syllabus is a Contract

If you expect your students to abide by the guidelines in your syllabus, then you are expected to abide by them too. This ensures fairness and consistency. For example, if your syllabus states that tests cannot be made up under any circumstance, then you must adhere to that rule. However it's best to allow yourself some flexibility in the wording of the syllabus. For example:

Tests can only be made up for the following reasons: serious illness of yourself or immediate family, jury duty, military duty, college athletic competition, or any other unavoidable circumstance that can be documented.

Personally, I do not consider "babysitter didn't show up" or "got called into work" as critical circumstances, and I state this in my discussion with the students. (Also include this in the Syllabus Quiz/Acknowledgement). In this modern world it's hard to predict all the misfortunes that can befall students. I once had a student call me from jail – he had been arrested for non-payment of child support and wanted to know if he could make up his test the following week. (I said yes.)

Beware of Ghost Students

Ghost students are a relatively recent (as of this writing in 2025) problem. A ghost student is formed when a fraudster submits a fabricated online application to a college or university and, upon acceptance, enrolls in classes. Once enrolled, the fraudster can exploit the fake identity to masquerade as a legitimate student. This allows them to misuse resources such as the institution's cloud storage, access a college-provided VPN, or leverage a .edu email address to carry out additional scams. In more severe instances, the ghost student's enrollment status is used to apply for and obtain significant sums of financial aid, potentially amounting to thousands of dollars. They then disappear (as ghosts are prone to do).

To prevent this phenomena, institutions can require some sort of visual identification and/or other verification measures. This year my college instituted a first week attendance requirement. For in person classes, students are automatically dropped if they don't show up in that first week. For web-based classes, students are expected to complete an assignment or activity.

The Wonders of Artificial Intelligence

Make sure the **spelling and grammar** of your syllabus are correct! Use AI to proofread and rewrite if necessary. Here's an example of a poorly worded paragraph:

> *You will have to do the following asignments: computer programming, oral presentation, report, questions in the textbook. Late work will be penalized. You will also have tests. If you're tardy I will deduct points.*

Imagine you're a student. Is everything crystal clear to you? How about the spelling?

Now, paste the following instructions in ChatGPT:

> *Analyze and rewrite the following syllabus paragraph: [followed by the above paragraph]*

In less than two seconds, ChatGPT returns the following analysis:

Issues Identified:

1. **Lack of Detail:** The paragraph provides a list of assignments but does not explain the nature, scope, or due dates for these tasks.
2. **Ambiguous Penalties:** The phrase "Late work will be penalized" is vague and does not specify the extent of the penalties or the criteria.
3. **General Statements:** The mention of tests and tardiness deductions is too general. There is no information about the frequency or weight of tests or how points will be deducted for tardiness.
4. **Informal Tone:** The wording is informal ("You will have to do"), which might not convey the necessary academic seriousness and clarity expected in a syllabus.
5. **Unclear Policies:** The policies for late work and tardiness lack specifics and structure, leading to potential misunderstandings.

Rewritten Paragraph:

Assignments and Assessments: During the course, you will complete the following assignments:

- **Computer Programming Project:** Due Week 5. This project will involve developing a software application based on the principles covered in the lectures. Detailed instructions and grading rubrics will be provided in Week 2.
- **Oral Presentation:** Scheduled for Week 10. Each student will deliver a 10-minute presentation on a topic related to current trends in computer science. Topics must be approved by Week 8.
- **Research Report:** Due Week 12. A 5-page report analyzing a specific area of computer science. Topics and guidelines will be provided in Week 7.
- **Textbook Questions:** Weekly submissions. Complete and submit answers to assigned textbook questions every Monday by 11:59 PM.

Late Work Policy: Assignments submitted past the due date will incur a penalty of 10% per day, up to a maximum of 50%. Assignments more than 5 days late will not be accepted without prior approval. Exceptions may be granted for documented emergencies.

Tests: There will be two major tests: a Midterm in Week 6 and a Final Exam in Week 15. These tests will assess your understanding of the key concepts covered throughout the course.

Tardiness Policy: Points will be deducted for tardiness in class. If you arrive more than 10 minutes late to a class session or presentation, 2% will be deducted from your final grade for each occurrence. Exceptions may be made in cases of documented emergencies or pre-approved absences.

Key Improvements:

- **Detailed Assignments:** Specifies the nature, deadlines, and expectations for each assignment, providing clear guidance for students.
- **Clear Late Work Policy:** Outlines specific penalties for late submissions, creating a fair and transparent system.
- **Structured Test Information:** Provides detailed information about the timing and purpose of the tests, helping students prepare effectively.
- **Precise Tardiness Policy:** Defines the consequences of tardiness, including the specific penalty and conditions for exceptions.
- **Formal and Clear Tone:** Uses a professional and academic tone that clarifies expectations and policies for the course.

Need I say more?

More on Assessment and Grading

"If you fail to plan, you plan to fail."

Assessment and Grading form the foundation of your course. It is critical that you include the number, nature, and due dates of assignments in your syllabus so that students can plan their semester. Keep in mind that most of your students are juggling more than one course. The number and nature of assignments should be geared to the level of the course (lower division, upper division, graduate level) and the level of students in your course.

For example, I would not have the same expectations for a College Algebra course that I would have for a Differential Equations course.

Do not burden your students with meaningless assignments. Your goals for the students are mastery, retention, and quality of work. The federal credit hour rule is one hour of classroom instruction plus two hours of work outside the classroom per week. So for a 3 credit course, the student will receive 3 hours of instruction and up to 6 hours of homework per week. Evaluate whether the full 6 hours is reasonable and necessary for mastery of your course objectives.

Assessment options and strategies for college instructors encompass a range of methods to evaluate student learning, provide feedback, and improve teaching effectiveness. They can be broadly categorized into **formative** and **summative** assessments, each serving distinct purposes in the educational process.

Assessment Options

1. **Exams and Quizzes**

   - **Types:** Multiple-choice, short-answer, essay, true/false.
   - **Purpose:** Evaluate comprehension and retention of course material, assess critical thinking and problem-solving skills.
   - **Frequency:** Midterms, finals, regular quizzes.
   - **Special Considerations:** Are make-up exams allowed? Do you drop the lowest grade? Do you allow re-takes?

2. **Assignments and Homework**

   - **Types:** Problem sets, research papers, essays, reflections, case studies.
   - **Purpose:** Reinforce learning, encourage application of concepts, develop research and writing skills.
   - **Frequency:** Weekly or bi-weekly.
   - **Special Considerations:** Is late work accepted? If so, under what circumstances and is there a penalty?

3. **Projects and Presentations**

   - **Types:** Individual or group projects, oral presentations, poster sessions.
   - **Purpose:** Develop teamwork, communication, and in-depth understanding of specific topics.
   - **Frequency:** Midterm or end-of-term.

4. **Laboratory Reports**

- **Types:** Experimental design, data analysis, conclusion writing.
- **Purpose:** Apply theoretical knowledge in practical settings, enhance scientific writing skills.
- **Frequency:** Regularly, aligned with lab sessions.

5. **Portfolios**

- **Types:** Collections of student work over time, including drafts, final products, reflections.
- **Purpose:** Show progress and learning development, encourage self-reflection.
- **Frequency:** Collected throughout the term, reviewed at midterm and end-of-term.

6. **Participation and Attendance**

- **Types:** Class discussions, online forum posts, group activities.
- **Purpose:** Foster engagement, assess understanding and application of course material in discussions.
- **Frequency:** Ongoing.

7. **Peer Assessment**

- **Types:** Peer reviews of assignments, presentations, or group work.
- **Purpose:** Develop critical evaluation skills, provide diverse feedback perspectives.
- **Frequency:** Periodic, linked to specific assignments or activities.

8. **Self-Assessment**

- **Types:** Reflective essays, self-evaluation checklists.
- **Purpose:** Encourage self-reflection, identify areas for improvement.
- **Frequency:** Periodic, often midterm and end-of-term.

Assessment Strategies

1. **Clear Rubrics and Criteria**

   - **Description:** Provide detailed rubrics outlining grading criteria and performance expectations.
   - **Benefits:** Ensures transparency, helps students understand grading standards, and improves feedback consistency.

2. **Frequent Low-Stakes Assessments**

   - **Description:** Use regular quizzes, short assignments, or in-class activities.
   - **Benefits:** Encourages continuous learning, reduces anxiety associated with high-stakes exams, provides ongoing feedback.

3. **Varied Assessment Methods**

   - **Description:** Combine different types of assessments (e.g., quizzes, projects, participation).
   - **Benefits:** Accommodates diverse learning styles, provides a comprehensive evaluation of student understanding.

4. **Feedback Mechanisms**

   - **Description:** Offer timely and constructive feedback on assessments.
   - **Benefits:** Helps students understand their strengths and areas for improvement, enhances learning through iterative feedback.

5. **Formative Assessments**

   - **Description:** Assessments conducted during the learning process, such as draft reviews, progress reports, or in-class activities.

- **Benefits:** Allows instructors to adjust teaching strategies based on student needs, provides opportunities for students to improve before summative assessments.

6. **Summative Assessments**

- **Description:** Assessments conducted at the end of a learning period, such as final exams, projects, or portfolios.
- **Benefits:** Evaluate cumulative knowledge and skills, serve as a comprehensive measure of student learning outcomes.

7. **Technology Integration**

- **Description:** Use online platforms for quizzes, discussion forums, and assignments.
- **Benefits:** Streamlines assessment administration, facilitates diverse and interactive assessment formats, supports remote learning.

8. **Group Assessments**

- **Description:** Assign group projects, collaborative presentations, or team-based activities.
- **Benefits:** Develops teamwork and communication skills, mirrors real-world collaborative environments, allows peer learning.

9. **Authentic Assessments**

- **Description:** Assessments that mimic real-world challenges, such as case studies, simulations, or practical applications.
- **Benefits:** Provides practical relevance, enhances problem-solving and critical thinking skills, engages students in active learning.

10. **Adaptive Assessments**

- **Description:** Tailor assessments to individual student needs and learning progress, such as adaptive quizzes or personalized assignments.
- **Benefits:** Addresses diverse student abilities and learning paces, provides a more personalized learning experience.

Sample Assessment Strategy Plan

Assessment Type	Frequency	Weight	Description	Purpose
Quizzes	Weekly	20%	Short online quizzes on weekly readings and lectures.	Assess understanding of weekly material.
Midterm Exam	Week 8	25%	Combination of multiple-choice and essay questions covering the first half of the course.	Evaluate cumulative knowledge and critical thinking.
Research Paper	End of term (Draft Week 12, Final Week 15)	25%	In-depth research on a course-related topic, including proposal, draft, and final submission.	Develop research and writing skills.
Group Project	Weeks 10-14	15%	Collaborative project with a presentation	Enhance teamwork and communication skills.

Assessment Type	Frequency	Weight	Description	Purpose
			and written report.	
Participation	Ongoing	10%	Active participation in class discussions and online forums.	Foster engagement and assess application of knowledge.
Self-Assessment	Midterm and End of Term	5%	Reflective essay on learning progress and areas for improvement.	Encourage self-reflection and personal development.

Additional Considerations

- **Inclusivity:** Ensure assessments are accessible to all students, including those with disabilities.
- **Feedback Loop:** Use assessment results to inform and adapt teaching methods.
- **Academic Integrity:** Implement measures to uphold academic honesty, such as plagiarism checks and honor codes.
- **Continuous Improvement:** Regularly review and update assessment strategies based on student feedback and outcomes.

Effective assessment strategies provide a comprehensive view of student learning, support diverse educational goals, and enhance both teaching and learning experiences.

By meticulously planning your semester and remaining responsive to the needs of your students, you set the stage for a successful and impactful teaching experience. Your thoughtful preparation and dedication to continuous improvement contribute to a vibrant and effective learning environment, enhancing both your teaching and your students' academic journey.

CHAPTER 2 WORKSHEET

You can answer these questions with respect to all the courses in your teaching schedule, or with respect to a specific course.

1. What textbook and materials will be required?

2. Will you be using an LMS (Learning Management System)? (Your college or department may require this) If so, which one?

3. If you will be using an LMS, how will you organize it -- by weeks, units, topics, etc.?

4. Will you be using an OLP (Online Learning Platform)? If so, which one?

5. Does your college/department provide a Scope & Sequence, or are you responsible for preparing your own?

6. What type of assessments will you incorporate?

7. Describe your grading schema.

8. What is your policy on late work and missed tests?

9. If it is a synchronous web-based course, are students required to attend (online) and/or participate?

10. If it is an in-person course, are students required to attend? Will you address tardiness, and if so, how?

11. If it is a web-based course, how will tests be administered – in person or online? Does your college have a testing center that will proctor tests for you?

3: GETTING READY FOR THE FIRST DAY

Education is not the filling of a pail, but the lighting of a fire. — William Butler Yeats

Starting the semester strong begins with thorough preparation for your first day of teaching. Whether you're stepping into a physical classroom or launching an online course, getting ready involves familiarizing yourself with the essential tools and spaces that will shape the student learning experience.

For in-person classes, this means getting to know your classroom setup: its layout, available technology, and any potential logistical challenges. Understanding how to effectively use classroom resources, such as projectors, whiteboards, and seating arrangements, can significantly enhance your teaching and ensure smooth class operations.

In the context of online courses, your primary environment is the Learning Management System (LMS). Mastering the LMS will empower you to organize course materials, facilitate discussions, and manage assessments efficiently. This chapter provides a step-by-step guide to navigating and optimizing your classroom or LMS to create an engaging and supportive learning environment from day one.

By investing time in preparing your teaching space, whether physical or virtual, you can reduce first-day anxieties, build confidence, and set the tone for a productive and positive learning journey for your students.

Get to Know Your Classroom

If you will be teaching in person, visit each of your classrooms. The good news for those of you who taught high school previously: you do *not* have to decorate it. In fact, other instructors will be using that same classroom at various times, so you do not want to leave behind any personal property. This includes pencils, pens, dry erase markers, etc because they may not be there when you return.

What technology is available to you in the classroom? Possibilities include:

Smart Board - an interactive whiteboard that combines a computer, projector, and touch-sensitive surface to enable dynamic presentations, collaborative learning, and interactive content delivery. Find out from the Technology Department how to use it. They usually have student technicians who are more than happy to give you a demonstration.

Smart Monitor – an interactive PC monitor with digital pen, connected to a projector that displays on a mounted screen.

Computer Lab – provides individual computers for students. You may have the capability, as an instructor, to view and/or control what is on their screen. Establish that screens should be off when you are lecturing and requiring their full attention.

In the absence of a Smart Board/Monitor, if the classroom has a projector and screen, I provide my own "smart" set up. I connect my tablet device (such as iPad) via HDMI cable to the projector. Thus I can pull up pdf files on my tablet and annotate them with a smart pen (such as Apple pencil). This is then projected onto the screen in the classroom.

Whatever technology configuration you wish to use, try it out before the first day of class!

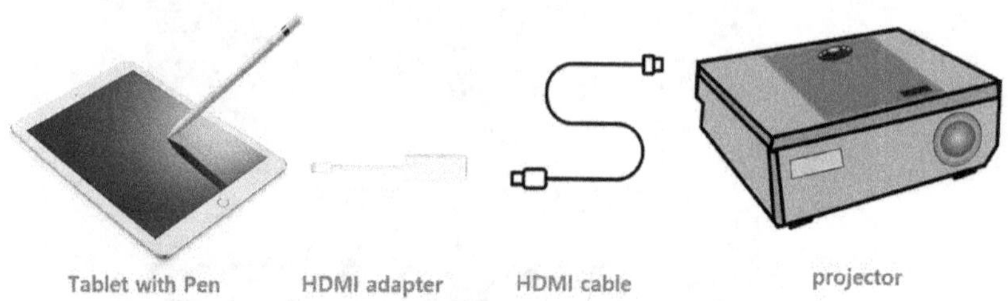

Or you may be old school and simply wish to write on the whiteboard. (Hopefully the college does not still utilize blackboards! White chalk is murder on dark clothes!)

Preparing the LMS

A **Learning Management System (LMS)** is a software application designed to facilitate the administration, documentation, tracking, reporting, automation, and delivery of educational courses, training programs, or learning and development programs. LMS platforms are commonly used in educational institutions and corporate environments to support e-learning and blended learning approaches.

Key Features of an LMS

Course Management

- **Content Delivery:** Hosts and delivers educational content such as videos, slides, documents, quizzes, and assignments.
- **Course Creation:** Allows instructors to create and organize course modules, lessons, and assessments.

User Management

- **Roles and Permissions:** Manages different user roles (e.g., student, instructor, administrator) with appropriate access levels.
- **Enrollment:** Handles the enrollment process for courses, including self-enrollment, batch enrollment, and integration with external systems.

Tracking and Reporting

- **Progress Monitoring:** Tracks learners' progress through course materials, assignment completion, and participation.
- **Analytics and Reports:** Generates detailed reports on learner performance, course completion rates, and overall engagement.

Assessment and Evaluation

- **Quizzes and Exams:** Supports various types of assessments including multiple-choice, essays, and practical tasks.
- **Grading:** Provides tools for automated and manual grading, grade book management, and feedback.

Collaboration Tools

- **Discussion Forums:** Facilitates communication and discussion among learners and instructors.
- **Chat and Messaging:** Offers real-time communication options for direct interaction.

Integration

- **External Tools:** Integrates with other educational tools and platforms such as video conferencing (e.g., Zoom), content repositories, and single sign-on (SSO) systems.
- **APIs:** Allows for integration with external applications and data sources via APIs.

Common LMS Platforms

Moodle

- **Open-source** and widely used in education.
- **Highly customizable** with numerous plugins and integrations.

Canvas

- **Cloud-based** LMS known for its intuitive interface.
- **Integrated tools** for grading, assignments, and collaboration.

Blackboard Learn

- **Feature-rich** with tools for both traditional and online learning.
- **Robust analytics** and reporting capabilities.

Google Classroom

- **Simple and free** for schools using Google Workspace for Education.
- **Integrates** seamlessly with other Google apps.

Brightspace by D2L

- **Scalable** LMS suitable for large educational institutions.
- **Advanced analytics** and personalized learning paths.

Edmodo

- **Social learning** platform with a focus on K-12 education.
- **Collaboration features** similar to social media platforms.

My college uses Canvas. Here is an example of the home page I set up for one of my courses.

WEEK 1 (6/17 - 6/22)

Here's a checklist for your first week.

1. Read the syllabus: ⌂ kauffman syllabus math 176.pdf ⬇

2. Take the Syllabus Quiz on Canvas: Syllabus Quiz and Acknowledgement due Sat 6/22

3. OPTIONAL: Print out the ⌂ section 1-1 note outline.pdf ⬇ and watch the lesson video at Section 1.1 video ⬀.

   Print out the ⌂ section 1-2 note outline.pdf ⬇ and watch the lesson video at Section 1.2 video ⬀.

   Print out the ⌂ section 1-3 note outline.pdf ⬇ and watch the lesson video at Section 1.3 video ⬀.

4. Create an account on XYZhomework.com. Use course ID **43132**. You will need to purchase an "All Access Pass" in order to complete the homework. Optional: Purchase All Access Pass bundled with paperback textbook. Both options are at: Applied Calculus for Business, Life, and Social Sciences by Burzynski, ISBN: 9781630983239 (xyztextbooks.com) ⬀

All Access Pass Purchased by Itself: $45.00
All Access Pass bundled with paperback textbook: $62.00

An ebook version of the text is included with your subscription to XYZhomework.

6. Complete first assignments on XYZhomework:

Section 1.1 - due Sat 6/22
Section 1.2 - due Wed 6/26
Section 1.3 - due Wed 6/26

As you can see, this is the Week 1 home page. Every week I update the home page. The Week 1 home page is the most important because

I am essentially setting the stage. You can see that I've included a list of upcoming assignments, helpful files, and information about the textbook and Online Learning Platform. Most of this is also covered in the Syllabus, but you want to make sure it's "front and center" every time they log into the LMS (which hopefully is often).

I know instructors who consider themselves "old school" – meaning they avoid anything having to do with technology. Without being too judgmental (okay just a little), these are probably people who still have land lines in their homes, outdoor antennas for their TV sets, don't know how to text, and still make use of the AOL email address they created forty years ago. They eschew the use of the LMS which is really a disservice to their students.

Welcome Email to Students

You will want to do this a few days in advance of the first day of classes. Many students like to be prepared in advance, or at least know what to expect. Many new students, especially high school students taking college classes, might not know where to log in or where to show up on the first day. Make sure everyone is prepared to start the semester prepared and confident.

Here's an example of an email I send to my students:

To: *[your college email address]*
From: *[your college email address]*
Bcc: *[list of student emails]*

Greetings Math 176! Our web-remote course starts Monday 6/17. I'm attaching a copy of the syllabus if you'd like to be prepared early. You should also be able to access the syllabus on Canvas. The home page of Canvas has a checklist of everything you need to do in Week 1.

Your homework will be submitted using a website called [*name of Online Learning Platform*]. You can create an account now using course ID 43132. There is a 15-day free trial; after that the cost is $45 for one year of unlimited access.

> Our class meetings will be held every Tuesday and Thursday from 10:00am – 11:50am using the zoom platform. You can download the zoom app to a tablet device, or go to zoom.us in a web browser. The meeting ID is always 985-932-9467. Keep in mind that attendance at the zoom sessions is 10% of your grade.
>
> Prior to each zoom meeting, I will post to the home page of Canvas a note outline in pdf file format. You will find it most useful if you print it out prior to the zoom meeting.
>
> Please let me know if you have any questions. I look forward to working with you!
>
> *[contact info]*

Of course if you'll be teaching an in-person class, you'll want to include the classroom location rather than the teleconferencing info.

You should be able to download a list of student emails from either the Student Registration Portal (such as **PeopleSoft**) or the LMS (such as **Canvas**). Make sure you paste the list of student emails in the **bcc:** section of the email header to protect their privacy.

Textbooks and Materials

Prior to the first week, make sure that the desired textbook and materials are available to the students. Many colleges use eFollett to carry instructors' textbooks.   The students can search for their textbooks by course number. Verify that your correct textbook and materials come up using this search method.

In particular, if you use a paid Online Learning Platform, make sure that the subscription offered is appropriate. For example, students will not need to purchase an annual subscription if the semester is only 16 weeks.

In summary, getting ready for the first day involves thorough preparation, creating a welcoming atmosphere, clear communication, engaging introductions, community building, practical logistics, encouraging a growth mindset, and being flexible. By focusing on these areas, you set the stage for a productive and positive semester, fostering an environment where students are motivated, engaged, and ready to learn.

Now it's time to do something relaxing for a few days so that you're mentally and physically refreshed for your first day of class!

CHAPTER 3 WORKSHEET

1. If you will be teaching in person, what technology does the classroom offer? (If you are teaching in more than one classroom, answer for each classroom.)

2. What LMS (Learning Management System) does your college use? What are its key features? How do you plan to use it?

3. What will you address in your welcome email to students?

4: PEDAGOGY

The mediocre teacher tells. The good teacher explains. The superior teacher demonstrates. The great teacher inspires. — William Arthur Ward

We have all seen movies about charismatic, inspirational teachers (*Dead Poet Society, Raiders of the Lost Ark, To Sir With Love, Dangerous Minds, Stand and Deliver*, to name a few). While most of these are based on real teachers, they are all – bottom line – screenwriter constructs designed to be dramatic and cinematic. Their dialogue and actions are designed to move the plot forward, and usually involve the teacher standing at the front of a class (or perhaps standing on a desk), delivering a rousing monologue about the subject matter (usually Liberal Arts), with row upon row of students staring in rapt, worshipful attention – so moved that they forget to take notes or look at the clock.

These movies always make teaching look easy, at least to those who believe they possess that same innate charisma.

It's not easy.

Simply being an expert in your field (armed with your Master's and/or PhD degrees) does not make you a good teacher. In fact, I venture to say it will make you a bad one. You will assume that all students are as brilliant and motivated as *you* were.

They are probably not. They need an instructor to meet them at their level, someone to present the content in an engaging, meaningful, and inspiring way; all the while building confidence. (Or at the very least make it palatable.) Which brings us to this:

> *What's more important than your subject expertise is your pedagogical expertise.*

CHAPTER 4

Pedagogy refers to the art and science of teaching. It encompasses the methods, strategies, and principles that educators use to facilitate learning and impart knowledge, skills, and attitudes to learners.

Pedagogy involves understanding how students learn and designing effective teaching approaches to enhance their educational experiences. It covers various aspects such as instructional techniques, curriculum development, classroom management, and assessment practices, and it can be adapted to suit different educational settings and learner needs. Several books have been written on the subject, which we encourage you to read. Our goal here is to provide you with key options and considerations to hit the ground running.

Key Elements of Pedagogy

- **Teaching Methods:** Various strategies and techniques used to deliver instruction, such as lectures, discussions, group work, and experiential learning. The focus of this chapter will be on teaching methods.

- **Curriculum Design:** The planning and organization of course content and learning activities.

- **Learning Theories:** Frameworks that guide how knowledge is acquired and retained, including behaviorism, constructivism, and cognitivism.

- **Assessment:** Tools and methods for evaluating student learning, such as tests, quizzes, projects, and formative assessments.

- **Learning Environment:** The physical or virtual space where learning takes place, including classroom setup, online platforms, and the overall atmosphere.

- **Differentiation:** Tailoring instruction to meet the diverse needs, abilities, and learning styles of students.

- **Student Engagement:** Techniques to motivate and involve students actively in their learning process.

- **Feedback:** Providing constructive responses to students' work to guide improvement and deepen understanding.

NOTE: Student Engagement should not be confused with Student Entertainment. You do not (and should not) need to dress in costume, play loud music or be a stand-up comedian to hold your students' attention. Unfortunately, you will most likely be tasked with educating a generation whose attention spans have been dramatically abbreviated by social media, video games, and virtual reality. Sustained attention and critical thinking may be new to them. Your first and perhaps most important task will be to acclimate them to a college classroom setting.

Bloom's Taxonomy

The topic of pedagogy alone is deserving of an entire book – of which many have already been written. I will therefore limit our discussion to the universal standard of human learning ... Bloom's Taxonomy.

Bloom's Taxonomy is a hierarchical classification system used to define and distinguish different levels of human cognition—in essence, the processes involved in learning. Developed in 1956 by educational psychologist Benjamin Bloom and his colleagues, the taxonomy provides a framework for educators to design curriculum, assessments, and instructional strategies that foster deeper learning and higher-order thinking skills.

Levels of Bloom's Taxonomy

1. **Remembering**
   - **Definition:** Recall basic facts, concepts, or information.
   - **Examples:** Listing, defining, naming, identifying.
   - **Verbs:** Recall, list, define, repeat.
2. **Understanding**
   - **Definition:** Comprehend the meaning of information.
   - **Examples:** Summarizing a concept, interpreting data, explaining ideas.
   - **Verbs:** Explain, summarize, describe, classify.
3. **Applying**

- o **Definition:** Use information in new situations or apply knowledge to solve problems.
- o **Examples:** Using formulas in math problems, applying theories to real-world scenarios.
- o **Verbs:** Use, apply, demonstrate, solve.

4. **Analyzing**
   - o **Definition:** Break down information into parts and examine relationships or patterns.
   - o **Examples:** Comparing and contrasting theories, analyzing arguments, identifying motives.
   - o **Verbs:** Analyze, compare, contrast, differentiate.
5. **Evaluating**
   - o **Definition:** Make judgments based on criteria and standards.
   - o **Examples:** Critiquing a piece of art, evaluating the validity of research.
   - o **Verbs:** Evaluate, judge, critique, recommend.
6. **Creating**
   - o **Definition:** Put elements together to form a new structure or original work.
   - o **Examples:** Designing a research study, writing a novel, creating a new product.
   - o **Verbs:** Create, design, construct, produce.

Applications of Bloom's Taxonomy

- **Curriculum Design:** Helps in creating learning objectives that progress from simple recall of facts to complex analysis and creation.
- **Assessment:** Provides a framework for designing assessments that measure different levels of cognitive skills.
- **Instruction:** Guides teachers in crafting activities and questions that challenge students at various cognitive levels, promoting deeper understanding and application of knowledge.

Benefits of Using Bloom's Taxonomy

- **Enhanced Learning:** Encourages comprehensive understanding and application of knowledge.

- **Differentiated Instruction:** Allows for tailoring lessons to meet diverse student needs by addressing different cognitive levels.
- **Skill Development:** Promotes higher-order thinking skills essential for problem-solving and creativity.

Example Use in Education

When designing a lesson on the Pythagorean Theorem:

- **Remembering:** Ask students to recall the formula.
- **Understanding:** Explain what the formula means and how it relates to right triangles.
- **Applying:** Solve problems using the formula.
- **Analyzing:** Compare different problems to identify patterns in their solutions.
- **Evaluating:** Judge the effectiveness of different problem-solving strategies.
- **Creating:** Have students create their own problems involving the Pythagorean Theorem and solve them.

Bloom's Taxonomy remains a foundational tool in education for structuring curriculum, instruction, and assessment to develop comprehensive and high-level cognitive skills.

Lesson Plans

Do not walk into a classroom, or begin an online lesson, with no clear plan of action. Your students will immediately sense your lack of preparation and wonder why they are expected to be prepared when you are not.

Unless your department requires a specific format, you can structure your lesson plans in whatever format reflects your teaching style.

A lesson plan is simply a description of:

A. The objective(s) you wish students to master in that lesson.

B. How you will enable that learning.

C. How you will check for understanding.

CHAPTER 4

You may wish to include time approximations for each event in your lesson plan. Here's an example from an introductory precalculus course.

Day: Monday	**Objective**: Use Pythagorean Theorem to Solve Right Triangles. Prerequisite Skills: Simplify radicals; distance formula
10 minutes	**Review** questions from homework
10 minutes	Students **work independently** on warm-up problems that involve simplifying radical expressions and using the distance formula to find the length of segments between points on the coordinate plane. Circulate through class and take attendance as students work on this.
5 minutes	Present Pythagorean Theorem; show animated **video** that demonstrates various proofs.
20 minutes	**Guided practice** in which instructor demonstrates how to find missing sides of right triangles.
10 minutes	**Independent practice** in which students solve the problems on their own, or in groups. Circulate through the classroom.
15 minutes	Present converse of Pythagorean Theorem. **Guided practice** in which students are given the coordinates of 3 points. Find lengths of the 3 line segments connecting these 3 points. Determine if the 3 line segments form a right triangle.
10 minutes	**Independent practice** in which students solve the problems on their own, or in groups. Circulate through the classroom.
5 minutes	Conclusion. Activity in which students summarize the lesson for themselves or another student. Questions?

As you become more experienced, you will no longer need to estimate the time for each lesson beat; it will become second nature. You may find it more useful to write out a note outline.

Publish Your Note Outline in Advance

Because I began teaching long before the internet (okay, back when math textbooks had tables of logarithms in the appendix), I got in the habit of writing everything out on the blackboard (which eventually was replaced by a whiteboard). I would write out an outline, then give the students time to copy the outline onto their notes. This is key – *give students time to write things down!*

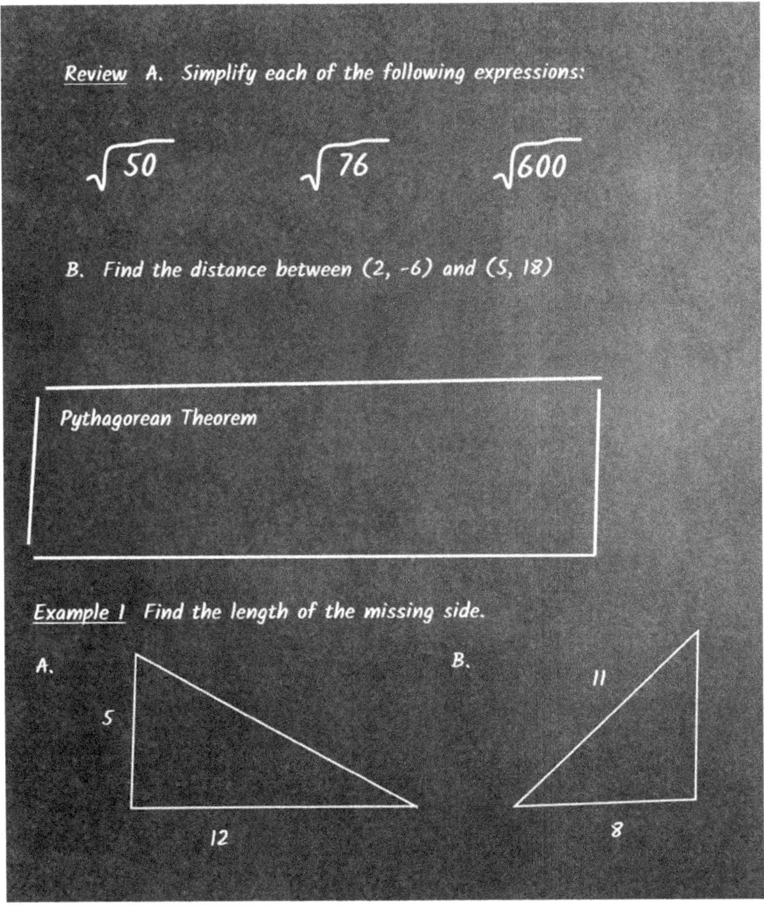

After filling in the answers, I would erase everything (the whole board!) and then write down the next section of the notes.

Eventually I realized that I could save a lot of time and make the students infinitely happier if I provided them with the note outline in advance. At the high school level, I would laboriously make xerox copies several days in advance and then hand them out at the beginning of class. Even the most distractible of students was able to follow along and fill in the blank spaces.

Of course you should not be spoon feeding college students to this extent. Simply upload the notes (as a pdf file) to the LMS a day or two in advance of the lesson. Make sure students are aware of where to find the notes online and encourage them to print them out.

Your class time is now spent filling in *answers* instead of waiting for them to copy down *questions*.

Using AI to Generate Lesson Plans

You may have heard the expression, "Don't reinvent the wheel." Artificial Intelligence, in the most superb fashion, can help you avoid reinventing the wheel. I gave ChatGPT the following prompt:

> *Write a lesson plan for a college algebra class with the objective to use the pythagorean theorem to solve right triangles.*

The result was immediate and comprehensive. It was also very similar to the lesson plan I previously described, so to vary the content, I added the next prompt:

> *Modify the lesson plan based on discovery learning.*

Again, the result was immediate, comprehensive, and appropriate. I will include this version of the lesson plan in Appendix E.

The art of giving ChatGPT instructions is called **Prompt Engineering**.

Examples

Mathematics (Calculus) - Topic: Chain Rule in Differentiation	*Create a lesson plan for teaching the Chain Rule in differentiation to college students. Include objectives, a step-by-step method for introducing the*

	concept, illustrative examples with complex functions, and applications in real-world contexts such as physics or engineering.
Literature (American Literature) - Topic: Analyzing Themes in 20th Century American Novels	Design a lesson plan for a college literature course focused on analyzing themes in 20th-century American novels. Outline how you will introduce a specific novel, guide students through the analysis of its themes, and incorporate multimedia resources and student-led discussions to deepen their understanding.
Science (Biology) - Topic: Cellular Respiration	Develop a lesson plan to teach cellular respiration to college biology students. Specify learning objectives, describe an engaging introduction to the topic, detail the processes involved (glycolysis, Krebs cycle, electron transport chain), and include a lab activity where students measure respiration rates in yeast or plant cells.
History (World History) - Topic: Causes and Effects of the Industrial Revolution	Construct a lesson plan for a college history class on the causes and effects of the Industrial Revolution. Include objectives, a lecture outline, primary source analysis activities, and a group project where students research and present on different impacts of the Industrial Revolution in various countries.
Business (Marketing) - Topic: Digital Marketing Strategies	Create a lesson plan for teaching digital marketing strategies in a college business course. Outline objectives, introduce key concepts like SEO, social media marketing, and content marketing, provide case studies for analysis, and design a project where

	students develop a digital marketing plan for a hypothetical or real business.

ChatGPT is not limited to entire lesson plans. It can be used to generate any part of a lesson plan, such as discussion questions, application problems, study guides, flash cards, writing prompts etc.

You are limited only by your imagination!

Assignments

An entire book could be written about how to craft challenging and meaningful assignments. There are uncountably many websites, usually specific to subject areas, that offer creative assignment ideas. Your colleagues can also share their best ideas with you.

But I would be remiss if I did not remind you about the wonders of AI. In addition to generating and refining Syllabi, Lesson Plans, Communications, etc., AI can also generate very precise and specific assignments for you. Here are a few examples of ChatGPT prompts in various subjects.

Mathematics	For an Introductory precalculus course, write *10 questions about sinusoidal functions involving amplitude, period, and vertical shift. Include application problems.*
English	*Write questions comparing and contrasting the works of Kurt Vonnegut and John Updike. Include all levels of Bloom's Taxonomy.*
Acting	*List 10 dramatic scenes from plays or movies for two student actors, in which the theme is racial injustice.*
Environmental Science:	*List 5 field study locations in Southern Nevada for college level students to investigate the water table.*

Philosophy	*Provide timely, thought-provoking philosophical questions or topics for debate.*

As of this writing, there are still many instructors (or society in general) who mistrust AI, perceive it as cheating, and generally feel it will lead to the downfall of civilization. At various times this level of mistrust was leveled against nuclear energy, television, the internet, calculators, computers, smart phones, genetic engineering, in vitro fertilization, and electric cars, to name a few.

However, using ChatGPT to generate creative ideas is akin to doing the same research via lengthy internet searches, perusing educational journals in one's field, or spending long hours in the library. AI delivers lightning-fast results catered to your precise needs – and with no annoying ads (as of this writing).

> AI is your free, virtual administrative assistant. Even better: It never complains and is exceedingly cheerful and polite at all hours of the day and night.

Services Available to Students

Your campus undoubtedly has a **Disability Resource Center** to assist students who need accommodations. Early in the semester you will be notified if you have any of these students in your courses, and to which accommodations they are entitled. (Examples: extra time on tests, quiet testing location, note-taker, etc.) These accommodations are not optional: you must follow them.

I usually inform students, when I am discussing the syllabus, that if they feel they may be in need of special accommodations, to make an appointment with the Disability Resource Center to find out what they need to be assessed.

Occasionally a student who is not registered with the Disability Resource Center may request an accommodation directly from you. They may tell you that their application is "in the works" or that their prior instructor(s) gave them special help such as allowing them to turn in late work, extra time on tests, etc. It is recommended that you do

NOT extend those favors. Other students, if they find out about it, could demand the same privileges, and your syllabus has just been rendered obsolete. The demanding student might make a similar demand of a subsequent instructor, arguing that a 'precedent' has been established.

Making Lessons Accessible to Students with Disabilities

Creating an inclusive learning environment for students with disabilities is essential for fostering equitable educational opportunities. You should be notified by your college's Disability Resource Center of students who require accommodations, and what those accommodations are. This is confidential information; do not call out the student in front of other students.

These accommodations are non-negotiable: it's Federal Law (the Americans with Disabilities Act (ADA) and Section 504 of the Rehabilitation Act.)

Here's a summary of effective strategies that college professors can implement to make their lessons more accessible:

Implement Universal Design for Learning (UDL)

- **Multiple Means of Engagement:** Offer various ways for students to engage with the material, such as lectures, discussions, and interactive activities.
- **Multiple Means of Representation:** Present information in diverse formats, including text, audio, video, and visual aids.
- **Multiple Means of Action and Expression:** Allow students to demonstrate their knowledge through different methods, such as written assignments, presentations, or projects.

Provide Accessible Materials

- **Accessible Documents:** Ensure all digital documents are compatible with screen readers. Use headings, alt text for images, and accessible file formats.
- **Captioned Media:** Provide captions or transcripts for all audio and video content.

- **Readable Fonts and Contrast:** Use clear fonts and high contrast between text and background to aid readability.

Accommodate Diverse Learning Needs

- **Flexible Assignment Deadlines:** Offer flexible deadlines for assignments when possible, especially for students with disabilities who may need more time.
- **Alternative Assessments:** Provide alternative assessment methods if traditional exams are not accessible for some students.
- **Note-Taking Assistance:** Arrange for note-taking services or allow recording of lectures for students who need them.

Design Inclusive Assessments

- **Accessible Formats:** Ensure exams and quizzes are available in accessible formats, such as large print or digital versions compatible with assistive technology.
- **Extended Time:** Provide extended time for assessments if needed, in accordance with documented accommodations.

Create an Inclusive Classroom Environment

- **Adapt Physical Space:** Ensure classroom layout is accessible, with clear pathways and appropriate seating for students with mobility impairments.
- **Interactive Technology:** Use accessible learning management systems and online tools that comply with accessibility standards.

Leverage Assistive Technologies

- **Adaptive Software:** Integrate assistive technologies like screen readers, speech-to-text software, and specialized learning apps into your teaching.

- **Lecture Recording:** Record lectures and provide them in accessible formats for students who may need to review material at their own pace.

Provide Clear and Detailed Instructions

- **Syllabus Clarity:** Clearly outline course expectations, assignments, and deadlines in your syllabus.
- **Structured Content:** Provide step-by-step instructions for assignments and activities, and repeat key points to reinforce understanding. (Notice that ChatGPT formats virtually all of its expository information in the form of an outline.)

Foster Open Communication

- **Office Hours:** Offer flexible office hours and alternative meeting times for students who may have difficulty attending during regular hours.
- **Feedback Channels:** Provide multiple channels for students to ask questions and give feedback, including email, discussion boards, and in-person meetings.

By incorporating these practices, college professors can significantly enhance the accessibility of their lessons, ensuring that all students have the opportunity to succeed.

Teaching Hacks

I have culled what I feel are the most useful tips for new (and vintage) instructors. This is not meant to be a comprehensive list. As you gain experience, you will develop (often by trial and error) successful teaching techniques that reflect your unique style.

I've organized these tips by the three course modalities: In Person courses, Synchronous Online courses, and Asynchronous Online courses.

In Person Courses

It is not likely, as a new hire, that you will be assigned a course in a vast lecture hall addressing a multitude of students.   I will therefore gear my suggestions to classes of 30 or so students.

- Learn students' names as quickly as possible. I use a seating chart app on my phone which also makes it easy to take attendance. It's a small gesture that goes a long way in making students feel welcome and valued.
- Take attendance whether it is included in the overall grade or not. At the end of the semester you may be required to provide the last date of attendance for students who fail.
- On the first day, find time to circulate the classroom to welcome each student. I do this as I fill out the seating chart app on my phone. Ask ask student how they would like you to address them. Do they have a nickname or other preferred name? A preferred pronoun? Make sure the students have a task to occupy them as you make the rounds, such as exchanging contact information with another student.
- Do not talk to the whiteboard. Face the students whenever you speak to them. Enunciate. Speak loud enough so that they can hear you in the back row.
- Whatever you write down – whether it's on a white board, smart board, computer monitor etc – write legibly.   Print, don't handwrite.
- Involve students as much as possible. The attention span of the current generation of students is about five minutes, or the length of a youtube video. (Or Tik-Tok, or whatever video platform is en vogue and not banned in your country.) To keep students on their figurative toes, I used to just throw out questions and then call on whomever raised their hand. But often, it was the same few students who raised their hands. To involve more students, I switched to the random student generator feature of my attendance app.
- Be sensitive to those students who are painfully shy or might not be able to answer your question when called on. I tell students

they can simply say "pass" or "come back to me later" if they don't wish to answer a question.

- Be kind if a student answers a question incorrectly. Try to rephrase the question in such a way that the answer will be more obvious.
- I always tell my students that I learn more from their questions than their answers. Your goal is to create an atmosphere in which students feel comfortable asking those questions. Sometimes someone will ask you a question that you don't know or recall. It's okay to tell them you don't know (*great question!*), but you will research it and get back to them in the next class.
- Stay on track. Yes, it's exciting when the lesson takes an interesting turn but don't spend excessive time pursuing tangents.
- Occasionally you have to modify the pacing of your schedule. You may have planned too much or too little. Sometimes the class needs more time to understand and practice a skill.
- Occasionally there is that "one student" who asks endless rudimentary questions to the point that the rest of the class grows restless and frustrated. (This arises often in **corequisite** courses in which students of wildly differing backgrounds are thrown into the same course and expected to learn at the same pace. For example, a student completely unable to perform operations with fractions finds themselves in a fast-paced Precalculus course.) When just a few students are slowing down the rest of the class, you're going to lose the class and fall off schedule. Perhaps you can ask to talk to them after class about available resources (your office hours, the college's free tutoring program, etc.) Alternately, defer certain questions to the end of class. Tell everyone that you will be holding 'lab time' the last 5 or 10 minutes of class for those who wish to stick around. No doubt the struggling student(s) will appreciate your personalized instruction at that time.
- We all make mistakes. It's okay to admit when you're wrong.
- Keep an eye on the time! Don't keep students past the scheduled end time.
- Occasionally you might finish early, having breezed through your planned material. Rather than just saying, "Okay we're

done for today, see you next time," rephrase it: "We've completed our objective(s) for today. I'm going to stay here if anyone wishes to stay for discussion (lab time, etc)." You are being paid to make yourself available to those students the entire scheduled time. It is unprofessional and indicative of poor planning to consistently end class early.

Synchronous Online Courses

A **synchronous online college class** is a live, interactive learning session conducted via the internet, where students and instructors participate simultaneously from different locations. This mode of instruction aims to replicate the real-time interaction of traditional in-person classes through the use of video conferencing and other digital tools.

Key Characteristics

- **Real-Time Interaction**
  - **Definition:** Both instructors and students are online at the same time, engaging in live discussions, lectures, and activities.
  - **Examples:** Virtual classroom discussions, live Q&A sessions, immediate feedback during exercises.

- **Scheduled Sessions**
    - **Definition:** Classes occur at specific times as scheduled, similar to in-person classes.
    - **Examples:** Weekly lectures every Monday at 10 AM, bi-weekly lab sessions on Wednesdays at 2 PM.
- **Digital Communication Tools**
    - **Definition:** Utilizes platforms and tools that facilitate live interaction.
    - **Examples:** Video conferencing software (e.g., Zoom, Microsoft Teams), chat functions, breakout rooms, shared whiteboards.
- **Engagement and Participation**
    - **Definition:** Active involvement is expected from students during the session.
    - **Examples:** Real-time polls, group discussions, live quizzes, collaborative document editing.
- **Immediate Feedback**
    - **Definition:** Instructors provide instant responses to student questions and work.
    - **Examples:** Addressing questions during a live lecture, providing real-time corrections on assignments.
- **Technological Requirements**
    - **Definition:** Both students and instructors need reliable internet access and suitable devices.
    - **Examples:** Computers or tablets with webcams, stable internet connections, microphones, and possibly additional software or apps for specific activities.

Examples of Engagement Tools and Strategies

- **Polls and Quizzes**
    - Use real-time polls or quizzes to assess understanding and keep students engaged.
    - Example Tools: Kahoot!, Poll Everywhere.
- **Breakout Rooms**
    - Divide students into smaller groups for discussions or collaborative tasks.
    - Example Tools: Zoom Breakout Rooms, Microsoft Teams Channels.

- **Interactive Whiteboards**
  - Collaboratively work on problems or brainstorm ideas on a digital whiteboard.
  - Example Tools: Miro, Google Jamboard.
- **Live Chat**
  - Enable side discussions and questions without interrupting the main lecture.
  - Example Tools: Zoom Chat, Microsoft Teams Chat.
- **Screen Sharing**
  - Demonstrate software, walk through presentations, or show solutions to problems.
  - Example Tools: Zoom Screen Share, Microsoft Teams Screen Share.

Challenges and Considerations

- **Technical Issues:** Reliable internet and functioning technology are crucial; any disruptions can affect the learning experience.
- **Time Zone Differences:** Scheduling can be complicated if students are in different time zones.
- **Engagement:** Maintaining student engagement in a virtual environment can be challenging.
- **Accessibility:** Ensure that all students have access to the necessary technology and that accommodations are available for those with disabilities.

The college may require that all instructors utilize the same teleconferencing platform, or you may be able to choose your own. If you wish to choose your own, here's a summary of the most popular **web conferencing apps** (as of this writing) that are widely used for online classes, meetings, and remote collaboration:

Comparison Table of Web Conferencing Apps

Feature	Zoom	Microsoft Teams	Google Meet	Cisco Webex	Skype	Slack
Max Participants	1,000	1,000+	250	1,000	50	15
Screen Sharing	Yes	Yes	Yes	Yes	Yes	Yes
Breakout Rooms	Yes	Yes	No	Yes	No	No
Recording	Yes	Yes	Yes	Yes	Yes	No
Chat	Yes	Yes	Yes	Yes	Yes	Yes
Integration	Wide	Microsoft 365	Google Workspace	Wide	Microsoft	Extensive
User Interface	Simple	Complex	Simple	Moderate	Simple	Moderate

You will also want to compare the subscription fees, and if your college will cover any of those costs.

It is worthwhile, in the week(s) before class, to acquaint yourself with the various features and settings of whichever software platform you will use.

Decide if, and how, you will monitor the students' engagement. It is human nature for a student to log in at the beginning of class, get distracted, and walk away from the session. (You may have done the same thing yourself in online meetings.) You can call on students randomly throughout the session; or you might include "Easter egg" questions throughout the session, then have students take a quiz immediately after.

You should also decide if you will record the sessions and make the recordings available at a later point for students who miss class or want to review the session. Keep in mind that students are capable of recording the sessions from their own computers using video capture software, whether you wish them to do this or not.

Asynchronous Online Courses

Asynchronous online college courses are educational programs where students engage with course materials and complete assignments on their own schedules, without the need for real-time interaction with instructors or classmates. This flexible learning model allows students to access content, participate in discussions, and submit work according to their convenience within set deadlines.

Key Characteristics

- **Flexible Scheduling**
  - **Definition:** Students access and engage with course materials at any time, providing flexibility to balance their studies with other commitments.
  - **Examples:** Watching recorded lectures at night, submitting assignments before a deadline, participating in forums over the weekend.
- **Self-Paced Learning**
  - **Definition:** Students can progress through the course at their own pace within the framework of the course schedule.
  - **Examples:** Revisiting complex materials multiple times, working ahead if they grasp the content quickly, or taking more time if needed.
- **Digital Course Materials**
  - **Definition:** Course content is provided online, including lectures, readings, videos, and other resources.
  - **Examples:** Pre-recorded video lectures, downloadable PDFs of textbooks, interactive simulations.
- **Independent Assignments**
  - **Definition:** Students complete assignments and assessments independently, often submitting work through an LMS (Learning Management System).
  - **Examples:** Writing essays, taking quizzes, participating in projects, or creating presentations.
- **Online Discussion and Collaboration**

- o **Definition:** Interaction with peers and instructors occurs asynchronously through forums, discussion boards, and group activities.
- o **Examples:** Posting responses to discussion prompts, peer reviews, group projects using collaborative tools like Google Docs.
- **Instructor Feedback**
  - o **Definition:** Instructors provide feedback on assignments and participate in discussions, though not in real time.
  - o **Examples:** Written feedback on submitted assignments, comments in discussion threads, periodic announcements or updates.

Typical Structure of an Asynchronous Online Course

Component	Description	Examples
Course Content	Organized into modules or units, each containing lectures and readings.	Weekly video lectures, reading assignments, case studies.
Assignments	Tasks and assessments to be completed and submitted by deadlines.	Essays, quizzes, projects, lab reports.
Discussion Boards	Platforms for student interaction and discussion on course topics.	Forum posts, peer responses, debates.
Feedback	Instructor comments on assignments and participation.	Written feedback, grades, rubric scores.
Assessments	Exams or quizzes to evaluate student understanding.	Multiple-choice tests, open-ended questions.
Office Hours	Scheduled times for students to ask questions asynchronously via email or discussion threads.	Weekly Q&A sessions, dedicated forum threads.

Examples of Learning Activities in Asynchronous Courses

- **Video Lectures**
  - o **Description:** Pre-recorded videos covering key course concepts.
  - o **Example Tools:** Panopto, Kaltura, YouTube.
  - o **Use Case:** Students watch and review lectures at their convenience.
- **Readings and Supplementary Materials**
  - o **Description:** Assigned texts, articles, and multimedia resources.
  - o **Example Tools:** eBooks, online articles, video tutorials.
  - o **Use Case:** Students read or view these materials to understand course topics.
- **Discussion Forums**
  - o **Description:** Asynchronous discussion platforms for student interaction.
  - o **Example Tools:** LMS forums (e.g., Canvas, Blackboard), dedicated class forums.
  - o **Use Case:** Students post responses to discussion prompts and interact with peers.
- **Quizzes and Exams**
  - o **Description:** Online assessments to test knowledge and understanding.
  - o **Example Tools:** LMS quiz tools, specialized assessment platforms.
  - o **Use Case:** Students complete quizzes by set deadlines to gauge their learning.
- **Projects and Assignments**
  - o **Description:** Independent or group tasks submitted through the LMS.
  - o **Example Tools:** Google Docs for collaboration, LMS assignment submission.
  - o **Use Case:** Students work on projects and submit them online for grading.

Challenges and Considerations

- **Time Management:** Requires students to be disciplined and manage their time effectively to meet deadlines without real-time reminders.
- **Lack of Immediate Feedback:** Students may have to wait for responses to questions and feedback on assignments.
- **Reduced Interaction:** Potential for a feeling of isolation due to less real-time interaction with peers and instructors.

Asynchronous online courses offer a flexible and accessible way to engage in higher education, making them ideal for diverse learning needs and lifestyles.

Recording Videos

In whatever modality your class is structured – in person, synchronous online, or asynchronous online – you may wish to supplement your course with pre-recorded videos that you make yourself.   Here is a brief comparison of the most popular screen recording software.

- **OBS Studio**: Best for advanced users needing comprehensive recording and streaming features.
- **Camtasia**: Ideal for professional video production with strong editing capabilities.
- **Screencast-O-Matic**: Balances functionality and ease of use, suitable for beginners.
- **Loom**: Perfect for quick, easy recording and instant sharing.
- **Snagit**: Excellent for creating annotated instructional content with both image and video capture.
- **Panopto**: Comprehensive video platform ideal for educational and enterprise settings, with robust management and integration features.

As with video conferencing software, you will want to compare prices and find out if your college provides any of these programs to its staff. Your video conferencing software might already include the capability to record sessions.

Choosing the right tool depends on the balance of recording needs, ease of captioning, and the level of integration required.

Grading

Time-Saving Grading Hacks for College Instructors

Use Rubrics

- **Consistent Criteria:** Create detailed rubrics with clear criteria and scoring guidelines for assignments and assessments.
- **Reusable Templates:** Develop reusable rubric templates for common types of assignments to avoid recreating them from scratch each time.
- **Student Awareness:** Share rubrics with students in advance to clarify expectations and reduce queries during grading.

Leverage Grading Software

- **Automated Grading Tools:** Use grading software like Gradescope, Canvas SpeedGrader, or Blackboard's Inline Grading to streamline the grading process. (Gradescope discussed more thoroughly in next section)
- **AI Assistance:** Utilize AI-assisted grading features to group similar answers and apply consistent scoring quickly.
- **Integrated Feedback:** Take advantage of integrated feedback tools within grading software to provide comments and annotations efficiently.

Create Clear Assignment Guidelines

- **Detailed Instructions:** Provide detailed instructions and examples for assignments to reduce student confusion and improve the quality of submissions.
- **FAQs:** Develop an FAQ document for common questions related to assignments and make it accessible to students.

Use Automated Tools for Objective Assessments

- **Multiple-Choice Scanners:** Use optical mark recognition (OMR) scanners or online quiz tools for automatically grading multiple-choice and other objective questions.
- **Learning Management Systems (LMS):** Utilize your LMS's capabilities to automatically grade quizzes, assignments, and discussion posts.

Implement Peer Review

- **Structured Peer Assessment:** Incorporate structured peer review processes for assignments, allowing students to provide preliminary feedback based on clear criteria.
- **Guidance and Rubrics:** Provide guidelines and rubrics for peer assessments to ensure constructive and fair evaluations.

Develop Standardized Feedback

- **Comment Banks:** Create a bank of commonly used comments and feedback phrases to quickly insert into student work.
- **Text Expanders:** Use text expansion tools (e.g., PhraseExpress, TextExpander) to quickly input frequently used feedback and comments.

Optimize Gradebook Setup

- **Weighted Categories:** Use weighted grading categories to simplify the calculation of final grades and reduce the need for manual adjustments.
- **Automated Calculations:** Take advantage of gradebook features that automatically calculate averages, totals, and weighted scores.

Streamline Late Submission Handling

- **Clear Policies:** Establish clear late submission policies and communicate them to students to minimize disputes and requests for extensions.

- **Late Submission Deductions:** Implement automatic point deductions for late submissions using your grading software or LMS.

Utilize Plagiarism Detection Tools

- **Integrated Tools:** Use integrated plagiarism detection tools (e.g., Turnitin, SafeAssign) to identify and address potential academic integrity issues efficiently.
- **Quick Analysis:** Use these tools for quick analysis of originality reports and to provide feedback on proper citation practices.

Delegate When Appropriate

- **Teaching Assistants (TAs):** Utilize TAs for initial grading, especially for large classes, with the instructor reviewing and providing final grades.
- **Grading Teams:** For collaborative assignments, consider using grading teams to distribute the workload among several instructors or TAs.

Grading Software

Grading software for college instructors helps streamline the evaluation process, manage student assessments, and provide feedback efficiently. I have tried to avoid promoting any specific online tool more than any other, but in this case I would be remiss if I didn't sing the praises of a website called **Gradescope.** I have no ties to Gradescope and get no commissions for recommending them. I would be just as happy to recommend any other grading website or software that has the same features.

I discovered Gradescope at the onset of the COVID-19 pandemic (March 2020), when in-person classes switched abruptly to online. Prior to that I administered, collected, and graded paper tests. (The homework was submitted online.) Now I was faced with how to have students submit tests, how I would grade them without breaking my printer, and how I would return the graded tests to students without spending hours scanning.

CHAPTER 4

Gradescope is a versatile grading platform designed to simplify grading for various types of assessments, including exams, homework, and coding assignments. Key features:

- **Flexible Grading:** Supports various question types (multiple choice, short answer, essays, programming).
- **AI-Assisted Grading:** Uses artificial intelligence to group similar answers for consistent grading and to streamline the grading process.
- **Rubrics:** Allows creation and use of detailed rubrics to ensure consistent grading and provide clear feedback.
- **Paper and Online Exams:** Accommodates both paper-based and online exams by allowing digital uploads of scanned student work.
- **Regrade Requests:** Offers a structured process for students to request regrading of specific questions.
- **Statistics and Reports:** Provides detailed analytics on grading patterns and student performance.

Here is how I use it.

1. At the beginning of the semester (or sometime prior to the first exam), I import the students' names to Gradescope.

2. For each exam, I upload a blank copy (in pdf format) to Gradescope. I identify the 'name' region on the first page, then identify the location of each question on each page.

Name

TEST 1 v1
MATH 176
Sections 1.1 – 1.3

DIRECTIONS: SHOW WORK WHENEVER POSSIBLE. Partial credit may be awarded for partially correct answers in which you show the correct steps. Points may be deducted for missing or nonsensical work. Do NOT use math-solving software or apps or you will receive a ZERO on the entire test. Good luck!

1. The following is the graph of the function f.

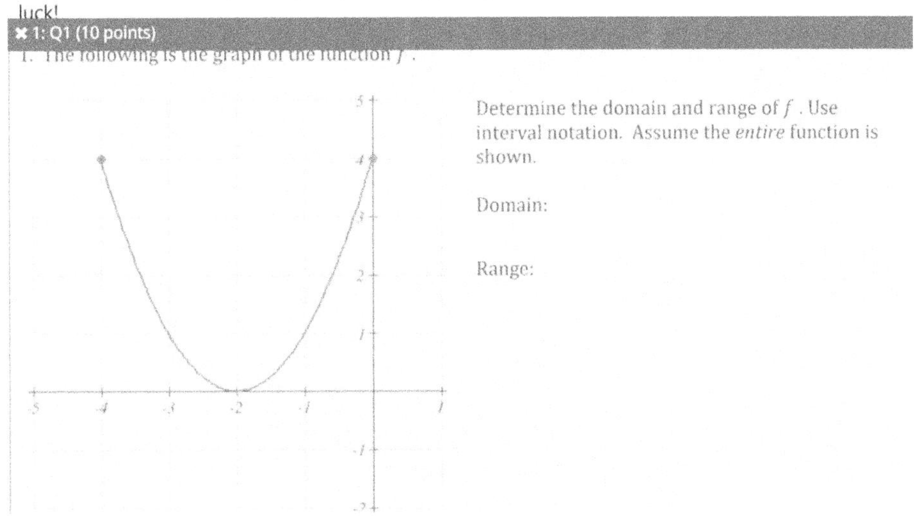

Determine the domain and range of f. Use interval notation. Assume the *entire* function is shown.

Domain:

Range:

3. At this step I can also set up a rubric for each question, or I can do that when I actually begin grading.

4. Students download a pdf version of the test from the LMS (such as Canvas). They fill it out, and when they are done, they upload it back to the LMS as a single pdf file.

5. I download all the tests to my computer, then upload them to Gradescope.

6. Gradescope performs handwriting recognition to try to identify the name of the student for each exam. (The results can be adjusted by the instructor.)

7. I then begin grading, one question at a time. After I set up the rubric, it is very easy to check off applicable rubric items and also give specific comments. What I like, as a math instructor, is that I can also upload an image of a graph or the steps leading to the correct answer.

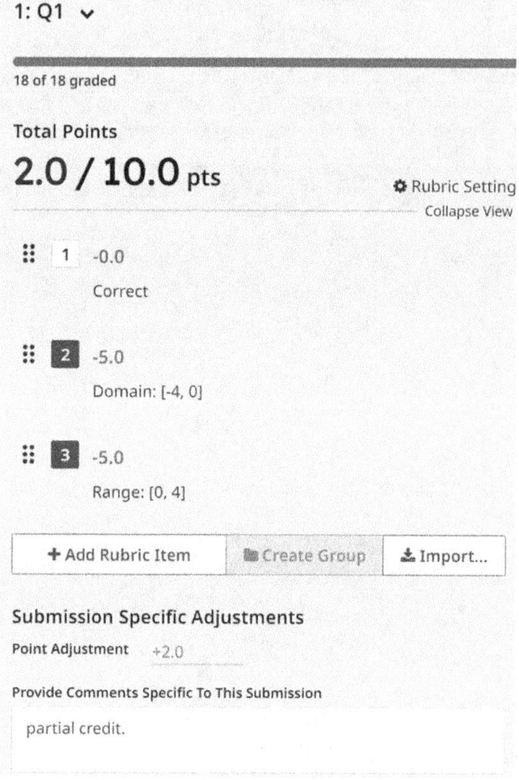

8. When all the tests are graded, I can then publish the grades, which sends an email to each student with instructions on how to log in and view their graded exam. If they would like me to review any of their answers, each question has a link for them to request I do so.

There are many options for you to personalize your grading routine. This is not limited to online classes. If you are teaching an in-person class, you can scan in students' tests using a scanning app on your cell phone.

Using ChatGPT to Assist with Grading College Homework

This section alone is worth the money you paid for this handbook. ChatGPT can assist with grading college homework by streamlining various aspects of the grading process, providing consistent and constructive feedback, and automating repetitive tasks. (No, I do not own stock in OpenAI.) Here's how ChatGPT can help:

Generating Feedback

- **Automated Comments:** ChatGPT can generate detailed comments based on grading rubrics or specific assignment criteria, helping provide personalized feedback for common mistakes or strengths.
- **General Feedback:** Create summary feedback for the entire class on common issues observed in homework submissions.
- **Constructive Criticism:** Offer suggestions for improvement and highlight areas where students performed well, based on input criteria or examples.

Creating Rubrics and Grading Templates

- **Rubric Development:** Help develop detailed rubrics for various types of assignments by outlining grading criteria and scoring guidelines.
- **Standardized Templates:** Generate standardized feedback templates that can be quickly adapted for individual student responses.

Evaluating Written Assignments

- **Content Analysis:** Analyze the content of written assignments to provide an assessment of argument quality, coherence, and structure.
- **Grammar and Style Checks:** Review grammar, punctuation, and style issues, and suggest corrections or improvements.

- **Plagiarism Detection Assistance:** Identify potential plagiarism by comparing text against a database of sources and highlighting matches.

Providing Exemplars and Explanations

- **Sample Answers:** Generate sample answers or model responses for comparison with student submissions.
- **Explanatory Notes:** Provide explanations or rationales for why certain answers are correct or incorrect, enhancing students' understanding.

Creating Custom Grading Algorithms

- **Rule-Based Grading:** Develop custom grading algorithms based on specific rules or criteria for assignments like coding projects or quantitative analysis.
- **Formulas and Calculations:** Assist with calculating grades based on predefined formulas or weightings.

Practical Examples of ChatGPT in Grading

ChatGPT is not restricted to evaluating essays. In computer programming, it can also analyze code submissions, identify software errors, suggest improvements, and provide comments on code efficiency and readability.

For math assignments, ChatGPT can verify solutions, provide step-by-step explanations for correct answers, and point out where students went wrong in their calculations.

As the human in this equation, you are responsible for verifying the accuracy of ChatGPT's work. I have found occasional errors in ChatGPT's math solutions.

By leveraging ChatGPT, college instructors can enhance the efficiency and consistency of their grading practices, provide more timely and detailed feedback, and focus on more complex and qualitative aspects of student evaluation.

Academic Integrity

Academic Integrity is the commitment to honesty, trust, fairness, respect, and responsibility in academic work. It forms the cornerstone of the educational process, ensuring that students' work accurately reflects their abilities and learning. Upholding academic integrity is crucial for maintaining the credibility of educational institutions and the value of their credentials. Unfortunately, in this digital age, the lack of Academic Integrity is becoming more and more common.

A 2023 survey by the International Center for Academic Integrity (academicintegrity.org) found that approximately 68% of undergraduates admitted to some form of cheating during their college careers. (Those are just the ones who admitted it.) The rise of digital tools has increased opportunities for academic dishonesty. In a 2022 study, 27% of students reported using technology to cheat.

The rise of online essay mills had led to an increase in contract cheating, where 15% of students have paid for assignments.

Your college undoubtedly has a formal written policy on Academic Dishonesty. Familiarize yourself with the steps to report a possible violation. At my college, there are a series of steps that involve:

1. Meeting with the student.
2. Submitting a form to the Academic Integrity committee, with supporting documentation.
3. The Academic Integrity committee will arrange a hearing with yourself and the student.
4. The Academic Integrity committee renders a decision and consequence.

Strategies for Preventing Academic Dishonesty

In addition to making sure that your syllabus clearly describes potential breaches of academic integrity and associated consequences, how else can you be proactive?

- Design assessments that require critical thinking and application of knowledge.
- Utilize plagiarism detection software (e.g., TurnItIn).

- Implement online proctoring services for online exams (e.g. ProctorU).
- When proctoring in person exams, circulate the classroom. Make sure electronic devices such as smart phones, smart watches etc. are put away. Use more than one version of the test. You may also want to make a diagram of where students are sitting relative to one another.

As a math professor with most of my courses online, the most common form of cheating is the use of math-solving apps to solve problems. One of the worst offenders is **PhotoMath** which allows students to simply take a photo of the problem with their phone; it then solves the problem and shows all the steps. Some of these steps are easy to identify as being from PhotoMath; as they are nothing like the steps demonstrated in class. In a Calculus class, I have caught students calculating derivatives using L'Hopital's Rule months before the rule is even learned.

Aha, you think, *I'll give them lots of application problems.* Not so fast - ChatGPT is very good at solving those application problems. (Very good but not infallible. I have noticed errors in Trigonometric and Linear Programming solutions.)

Be careful when confronting students – do not make overt accusations. You may be mistaken. Even if you are right, accusations usually result in defensiveness and more lying. Keep in mind that you are not "out to get" students who cheat. Think of it as a teaching opportunity – you want to help the student be more ethical and responsible.

Here is another situation in which you can use ChatGPT to your advantage. I gave ChatGPT the following prompt:

> *Compose a message to a student you suspect of cheating. Explain that you understand that they may not have understood that what they did constituted a breach of academic integrity. Give them the chance to admit their mistake and remedy the situation.*

The result:

Dear [Student's Name],

I am writing to discuss a matter of concern regarding the recent assignment/exam submitted for [Course Name]. After reviewing your work, I noticed some irregularities that may indicate a breach of our academic integrity policies.

I understand that academic integrity can be complex, and there may be instances where students inadvertently violate these standards without fully realizing it. It is possible that this situation arose from a misunderstanding or lack of clarity regarding proper conduct.

Therefore, I would like to offer you an opportunity to discuss this matter openly and honestly. If there was any misunderstanding or mistake, I believe in addressing it constructively and fairly. Please take this chance to reflect on the work you submitted and let me know if there is anything you would like to clarify or disclose about the situation.

I am available to meet with you to discuss this further and find a way to remedy the situation. Our primary goal is to ensure that all students understand the importance of academic integrity and have the support they need to adhere to it.

Please respond to this message by [Deadline Date] to schedule a time for us to meet or to provide your written explanation. I look forward to resolving this matter with your cooperation.

Thank you for your prompt attention to this important issue.

Best regards,
[Your Name]
[Your Title]
[Course Name]
[Your Contact Information]

CHAPTER 4

This approach fosters an open dialogue and encourages the student to take responsibility while maintaining a supportive and educational perspective.

In conclusion, effective pedagogy is the foundation of transformative education. As college instructors, our approach to teaching is pivotal in shaping students' academic journeys and lifelong learning habits. By integrating diverse teaching methodologies, fostering an inclusive and dynamic classroom environment, and continuously reflecting on and adapting our practices, we can meet the diverse needs of our students. Commitment to pedagogical excellence not only enhances student engagement and achievement but also enriches our professional growth and satisfaction as educators. As we navigate the evolving landscape of higher education, let us remain dedicated to upholding the principles of sound pedagogy, embracing innovation, and nurturing the intellectual and personal development of our students. Through intentional and reflective teaching practices, we can inspire, challenge, and support our students in realizing their full potential, ensuring they are well-equipped for the complexities of the modern world.

CHAPTER 4 WORKSHEET

1. Choose a learning objective in your field (e.g. *Students will be able to analyze the effects of climate change on global ecosystems and propose actionable solutions to mitigate its impact.)* Give an example of learning activities that incorporate each level of Bloom's Taxonomy.

2. Choose a learning objective. List the key features of a lesson plan that addresses the learning objective. (Do this without AI)

3. Use AI to list the key features of a lesson plan that addresses the learning objective you listed in #2. How does it compare to your answer?

4. What services does your college offer to students?

5. What activities will you incorporate to keep students engaged?

6. Write a teaching hack of your own.

7. What steps can you take to mitigate the use of AI and/or plagiarism in your course?

8. What is your college's procedure for addressing suspected breaches of academic integrity?

9. How will you personally address a suspected breach of academic integrity, before referring the matter to an institutional level?

5: PROFESSIONALISM

Reputation, reputation, reputation! O, I have lost my reputation! – Shakespeare, 'Othello'

As a new instructor, you are stepping into a role that demands not only expertise in your discipline but also a high standard of professionalism. Professionalism in academia encompasses a wide array of responsibilities and behaviors that contribute to a positive, respectful, and effective educational environment.

Professionalism is the cornerstone of successful academic practice, impacting everything from classroom management and interactions with colleagues to how you engage with students and represent the institution. It encompasses a commitment to ethical behavior, adherence to institutional policies, and a dedication to continuous improvement in your teaching methods and professional development.

Faculty Evaluation Form

Your college has a well-defined set of criteria to rate your professionalism: it is called the **Faculty Evaluation Form**. A sample copy is in Appendix F. Your college's Faculty Evaluation Form may or may not include the standards laid out in the sample; it may have additional standards.

You will have a formal evaluation/observation in your first year (usually in the Spring), and on a regular basis either annually or bi-annually after that. Typically, you will give yourself a self-rating in each standard (with a brief justification), and your department chair will also give you a rating and justification.

> *Don't wait for Spring to find out what is on the evaluation form. If it is not on the college's website, ask your department chairperson for a copy.*

The sample in Appendix F details these seven standards:

1. Syllabus Development & Presentation
2. Course Materials and Curricula Development
3. Content Presentation
4. Student Engagement and Participation
5. Evaluation of Student Learning
6. Student Communication and Support
7. Course Logistics, Proficiency, and Professionalism

Because the sample Faculty Evaluation Form in Appendix F is so thorough, I will not rehash every detail.   Rather, I will highlight those that warrant additional discussion and a few things not mentioned.

Meetings and Committees

Your school and department will hold regular **meetings,** usually monthly. These are not optional. In addition to discussing current issues and policies, meetings are an excellent opportunity to get to know your colleagues.   Do not be afraid to ask questions.   The department veterans will be more than happy to share their wisdom and experience.

A hallmark of college instruction is the opportunity to participate in committees and governance.   You may be asked directly by your department chair to participate in a specific committee, or he/she may put out a department-wide invitation to form or join a committee. You will want to participate in at least two committees in your first year, but don't overextend yourself. You will need time to plan and implement your curriculum.

College-Wide Committees

Faculty members often participate in various college-wide committees that address essential academic and administrative functions within the institution. These committees play a crucial role in governance, policy-making, and enhancing the educational experience for students and staff. Such committees may include Academic Affairs, Faculty Development, Student Affairs, Admission & Retention, Diversity & Inclusion, Research & Scholarship, Technology & Innovation, Ethics and Academic Integrity, Faculty Senate, and Curriculum Review.

Department-Wide Committees

At the department level, the key committees include Curriculum Development (including New Course Design and Textbook Selection), Assessment, and Faculty Search.

Continuing Education

Continuing education is vital for college instructors to stay current in their fields, improve their teaching practices, and meet evolving academic and professional standards. Various opportunities such as in-service training, conferences, seminars, and other professional development activities play a crucial role in enhancing instructional skills and academic knowledge.

In-Service Training refers to professional development programs provided by the educational institution where the instructors work. These are often mandatory and aimed at improving teaching skills, understanding institutional policies, and staying updated with educational technology and pedagogical strategies. These include workshops, orientation programs, and regular training sessions. Your college may have a website dedicated to in-service training opportunities.

Conferences are formal gatherings of professionals from specific fields or interdisciplinary areas. They provide platforms for presenting research, discussing trends, and networking with peers from other institutions. The various conferences for each subject are legion. Your department chair may mention a specific conference in a meeting or email. If you are very fortunate, your college/department may pay for the travel and conference registration. If so, this will involve an application to the college's Travel Committee.

You will also want to investigate **Academic and Professional Associations** and **Journals** in your field. If you are unable to attend conferences (or even if you can), these memberships will help you remain current in your subject and provide ideas for materials and instruction.

Continuing education is not only a pathway to personal and professional development but also a means to enhance the quality of education provided to students. By engaging in these activities, college instructors can remain at the forefront of their fields, continually improve their teaching methodologies, and contribute positively to the academic community.

Keep an ongoing **log** of all the activities in which you participate/attend: meetings, trainings, conferences, etc. When it's time to fill out your Faculty Evaluation form, you will be glad to have an easy reference.

Continuing Education not only enhances your expertise and keeps you informed about the latest trends and research but also provides valuable opportunities for professional growth and networking. These experiences can significantly contribute to your teaching effectiveness, research capabilities, and overall career development.

Establishing and Maintaining a Professional Image

It is important to establish and maintain a professional image from Day One.

CHAPTER 5

Dress Professionally - A good rule of thumb is to dress as though you are attending an afternoon wedding. Never been to one? I will be more specific: No jeans. Modest attire. Do men need to wear a suit and tie? Do women need to wear a dress? It depends. Err on the side of formality when you start teaching, until you've had a chance to observe how your colleagues dress for the classroom. If you are young(ish) – you especially need to draw a professional line between yourself and your students.

Speak and Act Professionally – Don't try to endear yourself to students by being hip. You can be friendly, but you are not their friend. Avoid using profanity – there are better ways to express yourself. Students are naturally curious and may ask you personal questions. Steer those questions back to the subject matter. Be careful with sarcasm and irony – some students may not "get it" or find you funny. Definitely avoid innuendo. This should go without saying, but don't insult your students. Do not disparage your college. (If you have issues, take it to Faculty Senate or the Union. Do not involve students.)

Always speak and act as though you are being recorded – because you just might be.

Political Neutrality – Maintaining political neutrality as a professor is essential for fostering a respectful, inclusive, and intellectually diverse learning environment. It ensures that all students feel comfortable expressing their views and engaging with course material without fear of bias or favoritism. Maintaining political neutrality has become more and more difficult in the United States, with the two main political parties almost on the verge of declaring war on one another. Keep your personal views private, and be respectful of students whom have opposite views. At the same time, you want to encourage critical thinking. Your diplomacy skills will definitely be put to the test!

What about campus advocacy groups? By all means, show your support. These are college sanctioned groups.

This brings us to the delicate subject of public protests on or off campus. You need to weigh whether the issue spurning the protest is worth losing your job. Absolutely steer clear of any protest that engages in illegal activity.

Political activism by college employees can lead to complex outcomes, influenced by institutional policies, public opinion, and the specific nature of the activism. There is a delicate balance between free speech and professional responsibilities in academia.

Online Confidentiality – Even prior to being hired, you should have set the privacy settings on all your social media accounts to the most restrictive level possible. Inappropriate photos and any content that at any point can be deemed as racist, sexist, sexual and/or politically incorrect can come back and haunt you. We have seen this play out over and over again in the news with public figures who posted the most idiotic things on social media.

Student Complaints

Resolving a student complaint effectively involves a structured, empathetic, and transparent approach to address the student's concerns while maintaining professionalism and adherence to institutional policies. Here's a step-by-step guide that college instructors can follow to resolve student complaints:

1. Acknowledge the Complaint Promptly

- **Listen Actively:** When a student approaches you with a complaint, give them your full attention and listen without interrupting. This demonstrates that you value their concerns.
- **Acknowledge Receipt:** Let the student know that their complaint has been heard and that you take it seriously.

2. Gather Relevant Information

- **Clarify Details:** Ask open-ended questions to understand the specifics of the complaint. Who, what, when, where, and how questions can help clarify the situation.
- **Document the Complaint:** Take detailed notes during the conversation to ensure all aspects of the complaint are recorded accurately.

3. Review Institutional Policies and Guidelines

- **Refer to Policies:** Check the college's policies and guidelines related to the issue. This can include academic regulations, codes of conduct, or procedures for handling complaints.

- **Understand Your Role:** Know your responsibilities and limitations in resolving the complaint within the context of these policies.

4. Analyze the Complaint

- **Assess the Situation:** Evaluate the complaint based on the information provided and consider the perspectives of all parties involved.
- **Seek Additional Input:** If needed, consult with colleagues, department chairs, or relevant administrative offices for advice or to gather additional context.

5. Develop a Resolution Plan

- **Identify Potential Solutions:** Think of possible ways to address the complaint that align with institutional policies and address the student's concerns.
- **Involve the Student:** Discuss potential resolutions with the student and get their input. This helps ensure the solution is fair and acceptable to them.

6. Communicate Clearly

- **Explain the Resolution:** Clearly communicate the proposed resolution to the student, explaining how it addresses their complaint and the rationale behind it.
- **Set Expectations:** Outline any steps the student or you need to take and provide a timeline for implementation. Make sure the student knows what to expect next.

7. Implement the Solution

- **Take Action:** Implement the agreed-upon solution promptly and follow through with any commitments made during the resolution process.
- **Document Actions:** Keep a record of the steps taken to resolve the complaint, including any communications and actions.

8. Follow Up

- **Check In:** Follow up with the student after a reasonable period to ensure that the resolution has been effective and that they are satisfied.
- **Offer Further Assistance:** Let the student know they can reach out if additional issues arise or if the solution needs further adjustment.

9. Reflect and Learn

- **Review the Process:** Reflect on how the complaint was handled and consider any lessons learned. This can help improve future complaint resolution processes.
- **Seek Feedback:** If appropriate, seek feedback from the student about how the complaint was resolved and any suggestions for improvement.

10. Maintain Confidentiality and Professionalism

- **Confidentiality:** Ensure the complaint is handled confidentially, sharing details only with those directly involved in the resolution process.
- **Professionalism:** Maintain a professional demeanor throughout the process, treating the student with respect and avoiding any personal biases.

Additional Context for Effective Complaint Resolution:

- **Remain Objective:** Approach the complaint without preconceived notions, aiming to understand and resolve the issue based on facts and institutional guidelines.
- **Resource Availability:** Be aware of additional resources, such as counseling services or academic support, that may assist in resolving the complaint.

By following these steps, college instructors can effectively resolve student complaints in a manner that is fair, transparent, and aligned with institutional policies, fostering a positive learning environment and maintaining trust with their students.

Now that you know how to establish and maintain an impeccable professional image, you're ready to start planning for tenure.

Tenure

Hopefully you have landed a **tenure-track contract.**

Tenure is a permanent academic appointment that provides college instructors with job security, academic freedom, and a stable career trajectory. It is a hallmark of higher education, designed to protect intellectual exploration and the pursuit of knowledge without the fear of job loss for controversial or unpopular ideas. Tenure allows instructors to pursue research, teaching, and publication without fear of being dismissed for their viewpoints, methodologies, or findings.

Tenured faculty have a permanent position, offering them job stability and long-term career prospects. The rigorous process of obtaining tenure ensures that only highly qualified and dedicated educators are granted this status, upholding the institution's academic standards.

The Tenure Process

1. **Probationary Period**:
    - **Duration**: Typically ranges from 5 to 7 years.
    - **Role**: Instructors are hired initially as tenure-track faculty and are evaluated on their performance in teaching, research, and service during this period.
2. **Evaluation Criteria**:
    - **Teaching Excellence**: Demonstrated through student evaluations, peer reviews, teaching innovations, and contributions to curriculum development.
    - **Research and Scholarship**: Assessed based on publications in reputable journals, books, presentations at conferences, and the impact of their research.
    - **Service**: Includes contributions to the institution, such as serving on committees, advising students, and participating in professional organizations.
3. **Review Process**:

- o **Peer Review**: Tenure candidates are evaluated by a committee of their peers who assess their teaching, research, and service contributions.
- o **External Review**: External experts may be invited to review the candidate's research and scholarship.
- o **Administrative Review**: Recommendations are forwarded to departmental chairs, deans, and often a provost or president, who make the final decision.
4. **Decision**:
- o **Awarding Tenure**: Successful candidates are granted tenure, securing their permanent position.
- o **Denial**: If tenure is not granted, the faculty member typically has a final year of employment to seek another position.

Reform and Alternatives

1. **Post-Tenure Review**:
- o **Periodic Evaluation**: Some institutions implement periodic reviews to ensure tenured faculty continue to meet performance standards.
2. **Contractual Appointments**:
- o **Fixed-Term Contracts**: Some colleges use renewable, fixed-term contracts that provide security but allow for regular performance evaluations and flexibility.
3. **Emerging Models**:
- o **Hybrid Systems**: Combining elements of tenure with more flexible, performance-based evaluations and career advancement opportunities.

Tenure for college instructors plays a crucial role in higher education by safeguarding academic freedom, ensuring job security, and maintaining high standards of teaching and research. The tenure process is rigorous, involving extensive evaluation of an instructor's contributions to teaching, scholarship, and service. While tenure offers significant benefits, it also comes with responsibilities and challenges that institutions must navigate. As the landscape of higher education evolves, the tenure system may continue to adapt, balancing the need for academic freedom with the demands for accountability and flexibility.

Essential Components of a College Instructor's Tenure Application

Applying for tenure is a pivotal moment in a college instructor's career, requiring a comprehensive and detailed presentation of their achievements and contributions. A strong tenure application typically includes evidence of excellence in teaching, research, and service. Here are the key components that should be included in a tenure application:

1. Personal Statement

- **Teaching Philosophy**: Describe your approach to teaching, including methods, objectives, and how you engage and support students.
- **Research Agenda**: Outline your research interests, key findings, and future directions.
- **Service Contributions**: Highlight your involvement in institutional service, professional organizations, and community outreach.

Tips: Be reflective and articulate how your work aligns with the institution's mission and values.

2. Curriculum Vitae (CV)

- **Education**: Degrees earned, institutions attended, and dates of graduation.
- **Academic Positions**: List of positions held, including titles, institutions, and dates.
- **Publications**: Books, journal articles, conference proceedings, and other scholarly works.
- **Teaching Experience**: Courses taught, including titles, levels, and semesters.
- **Service Activities**: Committee memberships, administrative roles, and contributions to professional organizations.
- **Honors and Awards**: Recognitions for teaching, research, and service.

3. Teaching Portfolio

- **Teaching Statement**: Your approach to teaching, including goals, strategies, and examples of innovative practices.
- **Course Materials**: Syllabi, assignments, exams, and examples of student work.
- **Student Evaluations**: Summaries of student feedback, including quantitative ratings and qualitative comments.
- **Peer Reviews**: Evaluations by colleagues of your teaching methods and effectiveness.
- **Teaching Awards**: Any honors or recognitions for teaching excellence.
- **Professional Development**: Participation in teaching workshops, seminars, or conferences.

4. Research Dossier

This is more important at the university level, and might not be required at the college level.

- **Research Statement**: Overview of your research agenda, major contributions, and future plans.
- **Publications**: Copies of published articles, book chapters, and conference papers.
- **Grants and Funding**: Details of research grants, including funding agencies, amounts, and project descriptions.
- **Citations and Impact**: Evidence of the impact of your work, such as citation counts, reviews, and mentions in other scholarly works.
- **Collaborations**: Description of collaborative research projects and partnerships.

5. Service Record

- **Institutional Service**: Involvement in departmental, college, or university committees and governance.
- **Professional Service**: Roles in professional organizations, such as leadership positions, conference organization, or journal editorial boards.

- **Community Engagement**: Outreach activities, public lectures, or involvement in local organizations related to your field.
- **Advising and Mentorship**: Mentoring of students, junior faculty, or colleagues. Include Letters of Reference you have written for students and colleagues.

6. External Letters of Recommendation

- **Selection**: Typically, external reviewers are respected scholars in your field who can provide objective assessments of your research and professional standing.
- **Letters**: Should address the significance of your contributions, the impact of your research, and your potential for continued growth and achievement.

7. Documentation of Achievements

- **Published Works**: Copies or links to your published articles, books, and other scholarly outputs.
- **Conference Presentations**: Abstracts, slides, or posters from conferences where you have presented your work.
- **Teaching Innovations**: Examples of new courses, curricular developments, or pedagogical tools you have created.
- **Service Contributions**: Evidence of service activities, such as committee reports, program development, or community initiatives.

8. Future Plans

- **Teaching**: Plans for course development, new teaching methods, or initiatives to enhance student learning.
- **Research**: Upcoming projects, potential publications, and new areas of inquiry.
- **Service**: Future roles or contributions to your institution, profession, or community.

9. Institution-Specific Requirements

- Carefully review and follow any specific instructions or criteria provided by your institution's tenure committee.

Preparing a tenure application requires a comprehensive and well-documented presentation of your professional achievements in teaching, research, and service. Each component should provide clear evidence of your contributions, align with institutional expectations, and reflect your ongoing commitment to academic excellence. By compiling a thorough and reflective application, you can effectively demonstrate your readiness for tenure and your potential for continued success and impact within the academic community.

Sabbatical

What do all these have in common:

- Conduct archival research in European libraries and archives to uncover new information about medieval trade routes and their socio-economic impacts.
- Perform a year-long ethnographic study in a major city to analyze how recent migration patterns affect urban communities.
- Conduct fieldwork in a biodiversity hotspot to study the habitat and behavior of an endangered species, and develop new conservation strategies.
- Work with international health organizations to design and implement programs for preventing infectious diseases in underdeveloped regions.
- Create a series of mixed media artworks that explore and raise awareness about the impact of climate change.
- Conduct research on the effects of cryptocurrency on global financial stability and investment strategies.

These are all examples of sabbatical projects in various fields of study, and all result in a written summary (or work of art) of the observations and conclusions.

A **sabbatical** is a paid leave granted to faculty members, typically every 6-7 years, to focus on research, creative projects, professional development, or other scholarly activities. It aims to rejuvenate faculty, enhance their expertise, and contribute to their academic fields.

The sabbatical gives the tenured professor time to conduct in-depth research, complete scholarly publications, embark on new academic projects, or engage in creative endeavors. It also provides time for intellectual rejuvenation, expoloration of new interests, and personal growth.

A professor is usually eligible to apply for sabbatical after 6-7 years of full-time service. The professor will need to demonstrate positive evaluations in teaching, research, and service.

The full-year sabbatical has a duration of one academic year. The compensation is often at half salary. The half-year sabbatical has a duration of one semester, typically at full salary.

The sabbatical is typically project-specific, i.e. the time is spent pursuing specific research or creative projects.

Application Process

Preparation:

Identify Objectives: Clearly define the purpose of your sabbatical and its benefits to your professional growth and the institution. Define a realistic and achievable project within the sabbatical period.

Develop a Plan: Outline your project, including goals, timelines, and expected outcomes. Set clear, specific, and measurable goals, and seek feedback during the planning stage.

Application Submission:

- **Proposal:** Submit a detailed sabbatical proposal including:
  - **Project Description:** Explanation of what you plan to accomplish.
  - **Timeline:** Detailed schedule for the sabbatical period.
  - **Expected Outcomes:** Anticipated benefits to your research, teaching, or professional development.
  - **Budget (if applicable):** Estimated expenses if the sabbatical involves travel or other costs.

- **Supporting Documents:** Include your CV, previous sabbatical reports (if any), and endorsements from colleagues or department heads.

Review and Approval:

- **Departmental Review:** Initial evaluation by your department.
- **Institutional Review:** Further review by the college or university committee or administration.
- **Approval:** Based on the proposal's merit, alignment with institutional goals, and available resources.

Preparation and Implementation

Before the sabbatical, ensure teaching and administrative responsibilities are covered during your absence. Secure any additional funding or grants needed for your sabbatical activities.

During the sabbatical, stay focused: follow your proposed plan and adjust as necessary. Keep detailed records of your acitivities, progress, and achievements.

Establish a schedule that allows for dedicated work time and personal renewal.

After the Sabbatical

Submit a comprehensive report of your accomplishments, findings, and how they will benefit your teaching or research. Integrate your sabbatical outcomes into your teaching, and share your experiences with colleagues.

Sabbaticals offer diverse opportunities for faculty across various disciplines to advance their research, innovate in their fields, and contribute to their academic communities. By selecting and planning meaningful sabbatical projects, faculty can achieve significant professional and personal growth.

Employee Advocates

Navigating the various protections available to college instructors is essential for ensuring fair treatment, resolving disputes, and maintaining a positive working environment. This section outlines key protections, including the role of the **ombudsman** and the **union**.

Ombudsman

An ombudsman is an impartial, confidential resource within the institution who helps resolve workplace conflicts, address concerns, and ensure fair treatment. The ombudsman provides guidance, mediation, and advocacy for employees without taking sides.

Contact the ombudsman when facing conflict with colleagues or administration that cannot be resolved informally. The ombudsman can also provide confidential advice on sensitive issues like harassment, discrimination, or unfair treatment.

The Union

A **union** is an organized group that represents faculty members in negotiations with the institution's administration. The union advocates for the rights, working conditions, and benefits of its members, and provides support in resolving employment-related issues. Functions of the union include collective bargaining, grievance handling, advocacy, and member support (legal advice and representation).

Contact the union when you have questions or concerns about your employment contract, when you believe your rights under the contract have been violated, or when facing disciplinary actions.

Understanding Union Rules in Right-to-Work States

Right-to-work (RTW) laws are state-level regulations that prohibit mandatory union membership and payment of union dues as a condition of employment. These laws aim to provide workers the freedom to choose whether or not to join and financially support a union. Unions still have the right to represent all employees in a bargaining unit, regardless of membership status.

Employees have the right to join or refrain from joining a union without fear of retaliation or discrimination. Employees can file complaints with state labor boards or the National Labor Relations Board (NLRB) if they experience discrimination or retaliation related to union membership.

Additional Employee Protections

Legally, your college must guarantee a workplace free from discrimination based on race, gender, age, disability, sexual orientation, religion, or other protected characteristics. These federal laws are discussed in the next section.

Legal Issues

College instructors must navigate several key legal issues that impact their interactions with students, colleagues, and the institution. Understanding these laws is essential for maintaining compliance, ensuring student rights, and fostering a safe and respectful educational environment. Below is a brief overview of significant legal issues, including Title IX, FERPA, ADA, and intellectual property rights.

Title IX

Title IX of the Education Amendments of 1972 prohibits sex-based discrimination in any educational program or activity receiving federal financial assistance.

Key Aspects:

- **Sexual Harassment and Assault:** Instructors must report any incidents of sexual harassment or assault involving students or colleagues.
- **Gender Equity:** Ensuring equal opportunities for all genders in academic programs, athletics, and other school activities.
- **Training:** Instructors may be required to undergo regular training on Title IX policies and procedures.

Impact on Instructors:

- **Reporting Obligations:** Faculty are often considered "responsible employees" who must report Title IX violations to the designated Title IX coordinator.

- **Creating a Safe Environment:** Instructors should foster an inclusive, respectful, and non-discriminatory classroom environment.

FERPA (Family Educational Rights and Privacy Act)

The Family Educational Rights and Privacy Act (FERPA) protects the privacy of student education records and gives students certain rights regarding their records.

Key Aspects:

- **Confidentiality:** Instructors must protect the confidentiality of student records, such as grades, attendance, and personal information.
- **Access to Records:** Students have the right to access their education records and request corrections to inaccuracies.
- **Parental Rights:** Parents have certain rights to access their child's education records until the student turns 18 or attends a postsecondary institution.

Impact on Instructors:

- **Handling Records:** Proper management and secure handling of student records to ensure privacy.
- **Information Sharing:** Avoid sharing student information without written consent from the student, except in specific, legally permitted situations.

Americans with Disabilities Act (ADA)

The Americans with Disabilities Act (ADA) prohibits discrimination against individuals with disabilities in all areas of public life, including education.

Key Aspects:

- **Accessibility:** Ensuring that course materials, classrooms, and activities are accessible to students with disabilities.
- **Reasonable Accommodations:** Providing necessary accommodations, such as extended time on tests, note-taking assistance, or accessible technology.

Impact on Instructors:

- **Accommodation Requests:** Respond promptly and effectively to accommodation requests from students.
- **Inclusive Teaching:** Incorporate universal design principles to make learning accessible to all students.

Intellectual Property Rights

Intellectual property laws protect the rights of creators over their creations, including research, publications, and course materials.

Key Aspects:

- **Ownership:** Understanding who owns the intellectual property created by instructors, particularly in relation to institutional policies.
- **Use of Materials:** Properly using copyrighted materials in teaching, including adhering to fair use guidelines.

Impact on Instructors:

- **Creating Content:** Be aware of institutional policies regarding the ownership and use of instructional materials and research.
- **Copyright Compliance:** Ensure compliance with copyright laws when using third-party materials in courses.

Equal Employment Opportunity (EEO) and Non-Discrimination

EEO laws prohibit employment discrimination based on race, color, religion, sex, national origin, age, disability, or genetic information.

Key Aspects:

- **Non-Discrimination:** Ensuring hiring, promotion, and workplace practices are free from discrimination.
- **Harassment Policies:** Implementing and enforcing policies to prevent workplace harassment.

Impact on Instructors:

- **Fair Treatment:** Treat all students and colleagues fairly and without bias.
- **Reporting:** Report any instances of discrimination or harassment to the appropriate institutional authorities.

Navigating these legal issues is crucial for college instructors to ensure compliance, protect student rights, and create a positive educational environment. Staying informed about these laws and institutional policies helps instructors fulfill their responsibilities effectively and ethically.

In summary, professionalism encompasses a dedication to excellence, ethical conduct, effective communication, adaptability, collegiality, accountability, and work-life balance. By upholding these principles, you not only advance your career but also contribute to a vibrant and dynamic academic community. Remember, professionalism is an ongoing journey that evolves with experience, reflection, and a commitment to personal and professional growth. Embracing professionalism not only enhances your effectiveness as an instructor but also positively impacts your students, colleagues, and the broader educational community. Your commitment to these values will guide you toward a rewarding and impactful career in academia.

CHAPTER 5 WORKSHEET

1. What are the key features of your college's faculty evaluation process?

2. What meetings are required by your college/department?

3. Do you have a mentor? What is their role?

4. What are the key features of your college's tenure process?

5. With whom (individual or department) should you consult regarding the following concerns:

   - You are not sure whether to report your suspicions that a student may be in an abusive domestic situation.
   - You believe that another employee in your department is saying negative things about your abilities on social media.
   - You believe that you are being assigned to teach undesirable courses due to your political affiliation.
   - You are concerned that another instructor is denigrating the female students in his classroom with "humorous" remarks such as *She's blonde, what do you expect?*
   - You are not sure whether to share grade information with the parent of a 17-year-old student.

6. A student in your course provides an Accommodation Letter from the Student Disability Office. You feel that some of the accommodations are unnecessary and unfair, such as extra time on a test and recorded lectures. Can you ignore them?

6: SEMESTER WRAP-UP

Congratulations, you've made it to the end of the semester! As the semester draws to a close, your role as an instructor transitions into a crucial phase of reflection, assessment, and closure. Effective semester wrap-up not only supports students in understanding their progress but also provides valuable insights for enhancing your teaching practice in future semesters. By approaching this process with clarity and purpose, you can create a positive end-of-semester experience for your students and lay the groundwork for continuous improvement in your academic career.

Final Exams

Undoubtedly you will be administering final exams. First, find out if your department has a department-wide exam they want you to use. Alternately, they may provide a list of **assessment questions** that they require every instructor for that course to include on their own final exam. You will be reporting the results of the assessment questions at the conclusion of the semester. These questions provide valuable feedback both to yourself and to the department as to which objectives students have mastered, and which need additional attention in future classes.

If you have the autonomy to compose your own final exams, here are a few considerations:

- Will it be cumulative over the semester?
- In the week prior to the final exam, you will find out that 99% of your students claim to have (undiagnosed) test anxiety. Will you be providing a 'Practice Final' and/or 'Study Guide' to students? If you provide a Study Guide, I recommend providing the outline only – it is the student's responsibility to complete the outline.
- Will students be allowed to use any type of notes during the exam? (Personally, I allow my students to use one 8.5" x 11" page of handwritten notes, front and back, because it alleviates test anxiety and helps focus their preparation.)
- It is tempting to get carried away and include questions on every single topic covered in the course. Don't overwhelm students. Make sure they can complete the test in the allotted time. If you are not sure, ask other instructors teaching the same course if you can view their final exams.
- Make sure the instructions are very clear. Here is an example of the instructions I include on my final exams:
  Directions: Show all your steps. Points may be deducted for missing or nonsensical steps, even if the final answer is correct. Partial credit may be awarded for partially correct work, even if the final answer is incorrect. Do not use any software or math-solving apps as this is considered a breach of the college's Academic Integrity policy and you will receive a zero. Good luck!
- Recommended: Use more than one version of the exam.
- If you are teaching an online course, either synchronous or asynchronous, will students be taking the final exam at home or will you require them to show up in person for a proctored exam? (If the latter, make sure it is stated in the syllabus and that you remind students often about the exam being in person.)
- If the Final Exam will be taken at home, will you require students to use an online proctoring service such as ProctorU? Your college

may have an agreement with such an online proctoring service so that you do not need to pay a fee. In brief, these services require students to have a camera attached to their computer so that a remote proctor can watch them during the test.

- If the Final Exam will be taken at home, will all students be required to take the exam during the same time window (such as 8:00am – 11:00am on Friday), or will they have more flexibility (such as anytime Thursday or Friday)?
- Will you be posting the answer key(s) online after the exam? If so, be aware that students can download and post your final exam to any number of websites that curate a repository of exams from instructors around the world.
- In consideration of the previous bullet point, do not use the same final exam in a subsequent semester.
- What is your policy about students who miss the test, whether in person or online? Even if your syllabus explicitly forbids make-up exams, you will be faced with students with all manner of last minute unavoidable tragedies, usually involving hospitalizations and/or funerals. You want to discourage fabrications and exaggerations but yet you don't want to fail a student who was maintaining a decent grade prior to the final exam. (Or do you?) My own policy is to give the student an 'incomplete' grade and then have them make it up in the college's testing center at the beginning of the next semester. This provides both a solution and (hopefully) a deterrent.

Grading Issues

Your grades should be calculated according to the grading scale in your syllabus. Period. Occasionally, after the final exam is taken, a student may contact you to ask for some last minute **extra credit** to salvage their grade. These requests, usually in the form of an email composed by ChatGPT ("I hope this email finds you well ...") can be persuasive and articulate.

First, ask yourself if this is fair to all students in the class. Will everyone be informed and offered the same opportunity for extra credit? Secondly, do you have time to devise and grade extra credit? Usually grades are due on the Wednesday following the last week of the semester. You may be grading final exams and calculating grades for 5-

6 courses. That leaves little time to contend with extra credit assignments.

Remind students that their overall grade in the class must reflect their mastery of the course objectives, and their ability to be successful in future courses that require such mastery. It is tempting to bump a "D" to a "C" for a student who claims they have a 4.0 GPA and how the "D" grade in your class will ruin their life. Ask yourself, does a grade of "C" accurately reflect their mastery of the course objectives? Are you actually doing the student a disfavor by sending them off to the next course in the sequence with deficient prerequisite knowledge?

These are all considerations when making and implementing your grading policies. It's a difficult balance to be both consistent and empathetic.

Entering Grades

As I mentioned, semester grades will be due within a week (usually Wednesday) after the last week of the semester. Do not make plans to go on vacation until your grades are entered. The grades will usually be entered online. For colleges that use PeopleSoft software (the student registration portal), your grades will be entered in that platform. For "F" grades, you may also be required to enter the last day of the student's attendance, which is why it is important to maintain accurate attendance whether you include it in the grade or not.

The **Last Day of Attendance** (LDA) for failing students is required for a variety of reasons that may include the college's refund policy, federal financial aid regulations, accreditation and compliance, scholarship requirements, and veterans' benefits. If you are teaching an online course, you may designate the LDA as the last day the student logged into the LMS, or the last day they submitted an assignment, etc.

Course Evaluation – Learning and Growing

Students will be given the opportunity to submit a course evaluation. You will be given access to their ratings and comments at the conclusion of the semester. It may be jarring to read criticism but for the most part students write positive comments. They also provide valuable suggestions that you may wish to incorporate in future classes. You may also wish to include the course evaluations in your tenure application.

Your department chair will also have access to the course evaluations.   Some department chairs consider these student evaluations when completing your annual Faculty Evaluation.

As we draw this handbook to a close, it is important to reflect on the core principles that guide a successful teaching journey at the collegiate level. This handbook has explored the multifaceted role of a college instructor, offering practical insights into pedagogy, professionalism, classroom management, and the myriad responsibilities that shape the educational experience.

Teaching in higher education is more than imparting knowledge; it is about inspiring critical thinking, fostering a collaborative learning environment, and nurturing the growth of future leaders. As an instructor, your commitment to continuous learning, adaptability, and empathy is crucial in addressing the evolving needs of students and the academic community.

Remember that the impact of your work extends beyond the classroom. Each lecture, assignment, and interaction is an opportunity to influence and inspire students, contributing to their personal and professional development. Embrace the challenges and rewards of teaching with enthusiasm and dedication, and continue to seek out new ways to enhance your instructional strategies and engage with your students meaningfully.

Thank you for your dedication to the noble endeavor of teaching. May this handbook serve as a valuable resource in your journey to becoming an effective and inspiring educator, guiding you toward a fulfilling and impactful career in academia.

APPENDIX A: GETTING HIRED

Securing a position as a college instructor involves strategic preparation, showcasing your expertise, and demonstrating your commitment to teaching and research.

The Job Description

There are many online resources for finding college job openings in your subject, such as HigherEdJobs.com, ChronicleVitae.com, and AcademicPositions.com. If you are interested in a specific college or geographic area, then visit the job listings in the Human Resources section of the desired college/location.

Read the job description carefully. It will describe the minimum and preferred qualifications, responsibilities, and required documents, for example:

- Resume/CV to be uploaded at the beginning of your application in the Candidate Profile under "Resume/CV"
- Name and contact information for 3 professional references to be entered into Candidate Profile. Letters of Recommendation will be collected by HR for those selected as final candidates.
- Cover letter to be typed/pasted at the end of your application to be uploaded at the beginning of your application in the Candidate Profile
- Research Statement to be uploaded at the beginning of your application in the Candidate Profile
- Teaching Philosophy to be uploaded at the beginning of your application in the Candidate Profile

As this is no small task, do not procrastinate! Get your application materials submitted well in advance of the deadline.

Prepare a Compelling Application

Craft a Strong CV/Resume:

- Highlight your educational background, teaching experience, research achievements, and relevant skills.
- Tailor your CV or resume to the specific job by emphasizing qualifications that align with the institution's needs.

Write a Persuasive Cover Letter:

- **Personalize** your cover letter for each application, explaining why you are a good fit for the position and institution. I cannot emphasize this enough: your cover letter should address every item mentioned in the job description. For example, if the job description mentions familiarity with diverse student backgrounds, discuss your relevant experience. Now is not the time to be modest. Run the cover letter through ChatGPT for a polish.
- Showcase your passion for teaching, your research interests, and how your background aligns with the institution's mission and values.

Develop a Teaching Philosophy Statement:

- Articulate your teaching philosophy, including your approach to student engagement, assessment, and inclusive practices.
- Provide examples of how you have implemented your teaching philosophy in previous roles.

Prepare a Research Statement (if applicable):

- Outline your research agenda, past contributions, and future research goals.
- Highlight how your research complements your teaching and benefits the institution.

Leverage Online Presence:

- Create a professional online profile on platforms like LinkedIn or academic networking sites.
- Share your research, publications, and teaching materials to build visibility and demonstrate your expertise.

Prepare for the Interview Process

Research the Institution:

- Understand the institution's mission, values, programs, and student demographics.
- Familiarize yourself with the department's faculty, curriculum, and ongoing projects.

Practice Your Interview Skills:

- Prepare to discuss your teaching philosophy, research, and how you can contribute to the department.
- Practice answering common interview questions and be ready to discuss your experience, skills, and future goals. Have someone else, preferably in education, do a mock interview with you.

Typical Interview Questions for a College Instructor Position

1. Can you tell us about your teaching philosophy?

2. Why do you want to teach at our institution?

3. How do you engage students in the learning process?

4. Can you give an example of how you handle classroom management?

5. How do you incorporate technology into your teaching?

6. How do you assess and grade student performance?

7. Describe a challenging teaching experience and how you handled it.

8. How do you stay current in your field and incorporate new developments into your teaching?

9. How do you support diversity and inclusion in your classroom?

10. What courses are you interested in teaching, and how would you develop them?

11. How do you handle feedback from students and colleagues?

12. Describe a time when you had to adapt your teaching to meet the needs of students.

Prepare a Teaching Demonstration:

- Be ready to deliver a teaching demonstration if requested, showcasing your ability to engage students and deliver content effectively. Include the relevance to students and society.
- Choose a topic that highlights your strengths and aligns with the course you might teach. Alternately, the interview committee may give you an impromptu topic.

- Practice! Incorporate technology if it adds to the topic. Include "handouts" for each member of the interview committee.

The Interview

For a full-time, tenure-track position, there will typically be 6-8 people on the interview committee. They will most likely take turns asking questions. Hopefully they will engage in a bit of chit chat to put you at ease. *("Where are you from?" "How was your flight?" etc.)*

- Dress professionally.
- When introduced to the interview committee: smile, make eye contact, firm handshake.
- If at all possible – remember and use their names.
- Speak clearly. Do not mumble.
- Demonstrate enthusiasm for your field. (It's a bit like auditioning for a TV game show, although it's not necessary to shout or jump up and down.)
- Do not assume that everyone has read your resume. Or perhaps they did, and forgot. Be prepared to reiterate your background information (education and experience).
- At the conclusion of the interview, when they ask if you have any questions, ask at least one meaningful question that indicates you did your research on their institution. Do **not** ask how much you will get paid – that's the purview of HR. I think it is fair to ask when you can expect to hear the outcome of the hiring process.
- Be sure to thank everyone for their time. Use their names if you remember them.
- There may be a second interview with the school and department chairs.
- My college also assigns another department member to give a personal tour of the campus, and treat the interviewee to lunch. (I can't guarantee that all colleges do that.)

A few days after the interview, you may wish to send a personal note to the department chair (or head of the interview committee) to thank them for the opportunity to interview.

Typically – and I know I use that word a lot – you will get a phone call from the department chair if you are hired, or a rejection letter from HR if you are not.

> *Don't be discouraged if you don't get hired. It doesn't mean they didn't like you. It means they did not have enough openings this year to offer you a position. I know several instructors who re-applied the subsequent year(s) and were eventually hired.*

By focusing on these strategies, you increase your chances of securing a rewarding position as a college instructor.

APPENDIX B: SAMPLE SALARY SCHEDULE

Each college publishes a salary schedule such as this one on their website. It is also of interest that many states have "transparent" websites that list the salary packages (including benefits) of public employees including educators, fire and police professionals, etc. For example, the website in Nevada is called www.TransparentNevada.com.

ACADEMIC SALARY SCHEDULE - STATE COLLEGE

RANK	TITLE	MINIMUM 9 MONTHS 12 MONTHS	Q1 9 MONTHS 12 MONTHS	MID 9 MONTHS 12 MONTHS	Q3 9 MONTHS 12 MONTHS	MAXIMUM 9 MONTHS 12 MONTHS
IV	PROFESSOR	$73,119 $87,742	$92,796 $111,355	$112,474 $134,969	$132,151 $158,582	$151,829 $182,195
III	ASSOCIATE PROFESSOR	$48,296 $57,955	$61,292 $73,550	$74,288 $89,146	$87,284 $104,741	$100,280 $120,336
II	ASSISTANT PROFESSOR	$43,939 $52,727	$55,780 $66,936	$67,622 $81,146	$79,464 $95,356	$91,305 $109,566
I	INSTRUCTOR	$42,343 $50,812	$53,762 $64,514	$65,180 $78,216	$76,598 $91,918	$88,017 $105,620

NOTE: For employees subject to the Employer-Paid Retirement Plan, the amounts shown will be reduced as provided by law.

ACADEMIC SALARY SCHEDULE-COMMUNITY COLLEGES

Grade	Min	Q1	Median	Q3	Max
5	$56,030	$68,267	$82,162	$98,871	$120,464
4	$52,294	$63,716	$76,685	$92,279	$112,433
3	$46,691	$56,889	$68,468	$82,392	$100,387
2	$41,088	$50,062	$60,252	$72,505	$88,340
1	$37,353	$45,511	$54,775	$65,914	$80,310

APPENDIX C: SAMPLE SCOPE & SEQUENCE

Example 1: U.S. History

Scope:

Content Coverage: Colonial America, Revolutionary War, Civil War, Industrialization, World Wars, Contemporary Issues.
Skills and Competencies: Historical analysis, critical thinking, primary source interpretation.
Learning Objectives: Understand major events in U.S. history, analyze causes and effects of historical events, evaluate historical sources.
Alignment with Standards: Aligns with state history standards.

Sequence:

Unit 1: Colonial America (Weeks 1-3)
- o Topics: Settlement patterns, colonial life, interactions with Native Americans.

Unit 2: Revolutionary War (Weeks 4-6)
- o Topics: Causes, key battles, Declaration of Independence.

Unit 3: Civil War (Weeks 7-9)
- o Topics: Slavery, sectional conflict, major battles, Reconstruction.

Unit 4: Industrialization (Weeks 10-12)
- o Topics: Industrial growth, urbanization, labor movements.

Unit 5: World Wars (Weeks 13-15)
- o Topics: Causes, major conflicts, global impact.

Unit 6: Contemporary Issues (Weeks 16-18)

- o Topics: Civil rights movement, technological advancements, modern political issues.

Example 2: Biology

Unit	Topics Covered	Weeks	Key Skills	Learning Objectives
1. Introduction to Biology	Scientific method, characteristics of life, cell theory	1-2	Scientific inquiry, observation	Define biology and its branches, explain the scientific method, identify characteristics of life, describe the cell theory.
2. Cell Structure and Function	Cell types, organelles, cell membrane, transport mechanisms	3-5	Microscopy, comparative analysis	Compare and contrast prokaryotic and eukaryotic cells, describe the functions of cell organelles, explain cell membrane structure and transport mechanisms.
3. Energy and Metabolism	Photosynthesis, cellular respiration, ATP, enzymes	6-8	Experimental design, data interpretation	Explain the processes of photosynthesis and cellular respiration, describe the role of ATP in energy transfer, understand enzyme function and factors affecting enzyme activity.
4. Genetics	Mendelian genetics, Punnett squares, DNA structure, genetic inheritance	9-11	Problem-solving, genetic analysis	Explain the principles of Mendelian genetics, use Punnett squares to predict genetic outcomes, describe the structure of DNA, understand patterns of inheritance.
5. Evolution	Natural selection, evidence of evolution, speciation	12-14	Critical analysis, evidence evaluation	Describe the principles of natural selection, analyze various types of evidence for evolution, explain mechanisms of speciation, and understand the impact of evolution on biodiversity.

Unit	Topics Covered	Weeks	Key Skills	Learning Objectives
. Ecology	Ecosystem structure, energy flow, biogeochemical cycles, population dynamics	15-16	Systems thinking, ecological modeling	Describe ecosystem components and energy flow, explain the roles of producers, consumers, and decomposers, understand biogeochemical cycles, analyze factors affecting population dynamics.
. Human Body Systems	Overview of major systems: circulatory, respiratory, digestive, nervous	18-20	Integration, physiological understanding	Identify the main organs and functions of the circulatory, respiratory, digestive, and nervous systems, explain the interdependence of these systems, understand basic physiological processes.

APPENDIX D: SAMPLE SYLLABUS

[COLLEGE NAME]
COURSE SYLLABUS

[COURSE NAME AND NUMBER]
[Semester, Section]
[Modality: In person, online]

INSTRUCTOR INFO

Instructor:
Office:
Phone:
Email:
Office Hours:

COURSE DESCRIPTION

[Description in college catalog, including prerequisites]

LEARNING OUTCOMES

[objectives as defined by department]

REQUIRED TEXT AND MATERIALS

[textbook name, ISBN]
[subscription to any homework platforms]

TECHNOLOGICAL AIDS

Your grades and assignments will be posted on the [name of college] website portal [URL of LMS]. It is recommended you set notifications so that course announcements, grades, assignments etc. are texted to your mobile phone.

For computer issues, the Help Desk can be reached at [phone].
[calculator policy, if relevant]
[other materials and where they can be obtained]

GRADES

Assignments   30%
Tests (3)   30%
Final Exam   30%
TOTAL   100%

Grading Scale:
89 – 100%   A
79 – 88.9%   B
69 – 78.9%   C
59 – 68.9%   D
0 – 58.9%   F

A "+" will be appended to the top 1% in each category, and a "-" grade to the lowest 1%. For example, if you score 89%, your grade will be an "A-". If you score 88%, your grade will be a "B+".

ASSIGNMENTS

Homework assignments will be completed on [URL of homework portal]. Homeworks are due on Wednesday and Saturday evenings. The [name of homework portal] will allow 2 late passes for 48 hours.

If you have a technical issue with [name of homework portal] that prevents you from completing the assignment by the deadline, then take a screenshot and email it to me as soon as the problem occurs. I can then extend your assignment deadline.

TESTS AND FINAL EXAM

In addition to the homework described above, there will be 3 Tests and a Final Exam. See the course schedule below for exact dates.

The tests will be "take home" tests which you will download from [name of LMS] (or copy onto a piece of paper), fill out, scan into a pdf file, then upload back to [name of LMS]. You can take each exam either Friday or Saturday of the indicated week. (see schedule below) If you are not available during that time period, you can take it Thursday of that week if you notify me in advance.

If you miss a test, then you can make up the test in person at one of the three testing centers within one week. Please make arrangements with me as soon as possible.

COURSE SCHEDULE

This is a rough timeline. Actual assignments and due dates will be on the [name of LMS] calendar.

Week	Dates	Sections	Quiz or Exam
1	6/17 – 6/22	1.1 – 1.3, Syllabus Quiz	

2	6/24 – 6/29	1.4 - 1.6	**TEST 1 (Fri or Sat)**
3	7/1 – 7/6	2.1 – 2.4	
4	7/8 – 7/13	2.5, 3.1, 3.3	**TEST 2 (Fri or Sat)**
5	7/15 – 7/20	3.4, 4.1 – 4.2	
6	7/22 – 7/28	4.3 – 4.4, 5.1	**TEST 3 (Fri or Sat)**
7	7/29 – 8/3	5.2 – 5.4	
8	8/5 – 8/10	6.1 – 6.2	**FINAL EXAM (Fri or Sat)**

ACADEMIC INTEGRITY POLICY

The [name of college] Academic Integrity Policy states that [name of college] students assume the obligation to conduct themselves with integrity in their academic pursuits. Academic dishonesty includes copying words, images and ideas from the internet; using unauthorized materials and electronic devices during examinations; using AI to complete work, or communication in any manner with someone else during an examination.

The consequences for violating the [name of college] Academic Integrity Policy include academic sanctions ranging from a failing grade on the assignment to a failing grade in the course, depending on the nature of the violation. Repeated schoolwide violations could result in suspension or expulsion from the college.

Full details of the [name of college] Academic Integrity Policy can be found at [URL].

STUDENTS WITH DISABILITIES

APPENDIX D

[name of college] is committed to making physical facilities and instructional programs accessible to students with disabilities. If you have a disability that may have some impact on your work in this class and for which you may require accommodations, please visit the Disability Resource Center (DRC) so that such accommodations can be considered. All discussions will remain confidential. The DRC has offices on all three campuses. These serve as the focal point for coordination of services for students with disabilities. If you have a physical, emotional, or mental disability that "substantially limits one or more major life activities (including walking, seeing, hearing, speaking, breathing, learning and working)," and will require accommodation in this class, please contact the DRC at [contact info]. For Deaf and Hard of Hearing Services contact the DRC using [phone], or email at [email].

CENTERS FOR ACADEMIC SUCCESS

[info about tutoring centers and online tutoring, including location(s), contact info, and hours.]

ADVISING

Advisor/Success Coaches help students assess academic strengths and limitations, learn academic success strategies, explore careers, declare a major, navigate the educational system, access campus and community resources, and connect to campus life. [Location(s), contact info, and hours]

COLLEGE RESOURCES

There are many free, helpful services for [name of college] students at all three campuses. These includes Advising and Coaching Services, Success Coaches, Academic Counseling, Career Services, Child Care, Computer Labs, Counseling and Psychological Services (CAPS), Deaf and Hard of Hearing Services, Disability Resource Center, Financial Aid, International Center, Language Labs, Library Services, Student Life and

Leadership Development, Testing and Assessment Centers, TRiO Student Support Services, Transfer Office, and Veteran Affairs. (Visit [URL] for more info)

College Counselors provide direct support and assistance for students on E-Alert, Academic   Warning, Academic   Probation, Academic Suspension, Financial Aid Warning, Financial Aid Suspension Appeals (SAP). Counselors also help with wrap around services (ex. Connecting students to on campus community agencies and resources, food pantry, emergency money fund, immigration lawyer, Workforce Connections, etc.) retention services and mentoring. Visit [URL] for more information or contact [contact info].

STUDENTS' RIGHTS AND RESPONSIBILITIES

When you choose to become a student at [name of college], you accept the rights and responsibilities of membership in [name of college]'s academic and social community. You can find policies covering students such as the Student Conduct, Students' Right to Know, Students' Academic Integrity, and Disruptive and Abusive Student in the following locations:

Catalog and Student Handbook: [URL] in the Policies and Procedures section.
[name of college] Website: [URL]

A good summary is the Golden Rule: Treat others as you wish to be treated.

Instructors have the responsibility to set and maintain standards of classroom behavior appropriate to the discipline and method of instruction. No objectionable materials or language will be used during this class. This includes all possible modes of the class: online and in person. The instructor will make the final determination regarding any objectionable materials or language. Students may not engage in activity the instructor deems disruptive or counterproductive to the goals of the class. Instructors have the right to remove offending students from class.

NON-DISCRIMINATION AND SEXUAL HARASSMENT POLICIES

[name of college] is committed to providing a place of work and learning free of discrimination on the basis of a person's age, disability, whether actual or perceived by others (including service-connected disabilities), gender (including pregnancy related condition), military status or military obligations, sexual orientation, gender identity or expression, genetic information, national origin, race, or religion. Where discrimination is found to have occurred, [name of college] will act to stop the discrimination, to prevent its recurrence, to remedy its effects, and to discipline those responsible.

[name of college] is committed to providing a place of work and learning free of sexual harassment, including sexual violence. Where sexual harassment is found to have occurred, [name of college] will act to stop the harassment, to prevent its recurrence, to remedy its effects, and to discipline those responsible in accordance with the [state code] or, in the case of classified employees, the [state code]. Sexual harassment, including sexual violence, is a form of discrimination; it is illegal. No employee or student, either in the workplace or in the academic environment, should be subject to unwelcome verbal or physical conduct that is sexual in nature. Sexual harassment does not refer to occasional compliments of a socially acceptable nature. It refers to behavior of a sexual nature that is not welcome, that is personally offensive, and that interferes with performance.

More information about the application of these policies (falling under the umbrella of the Federal Title IX Law), including how to file a complaint, can be found at the [name of college] Affirmative Action page: [URL]

STATEMENT OF SAFETY OR RISK ASSUMPTION

[name of college] maintains a comprehensive policy regarding environmental safety and health, emergency procedures, fire prevention and safety, and hazardous materials. Additionally, the [name of college] Police Department is responsible for providing security and protection services on all campuses. This includes a uniformed escort service to ensure additional safety after dark, to bus stop or vehicles, depending upon the availability of resources. Students, faculty and staff who need this service should call the appropriate Public Safety Offices at their campus location:
[contact info]
Emergency telephones are in most classrooms that connect directly to Campus Security.

The [name of college] Dept. of Public Safety is available 24-7, 365 days a year. See something, say something:

NON-Emergency:..............................[phone]
Emergency:...................................... [phone]

DISCLAIMERS

This syllabus is subject to change as deemed appropriate by the instructor with advance notification. An updated version of the syllabus is available on [LMS].

APPENDIX E:SAMPLE LESSON PLAN

Class Information

- **Course:** College Algebra
- **Lesson Title:** Discovering the Pythagorean Theorem to Solve Right Triangles
- **Duration:** 90 minutes
- **Instructor:** [Instructor's Name]

Objective

Students will discover and apply the Pythagorean Theorem through exploration and problem-solving activities to understand the relationship between the sides of right triangles.

Materials Needed

- Graph paper
- Rulers and protractors
- Scissors and glue
- Calculators
- Handouts with exploration activities
- Interactive geometry software (e.g., GeoGebra)
- Whiteboard or Smartboard
- Markers
- Projector and computer for visual aids

Lesson Outline

Time	Activity	Description	Materials
10 mins	Introduction	Welcome and take attendance. Introduce the day's topic and objective: discovering the Pythagorean Theorem.	None
15 mins	Exploration Activity 1	Hands-on exploration to discover the Pythagorean relationship by creating and measuring right triangles.	Graph paper Rulers Protractors
20 mins	Exploration Activity 2	Group activity using interactive geometry software to visualize and verify the Pythagorean Theorem.	Computers GeoGebra
15 mins	Guided Discovery	Facilitate a discussion where students share findings and develop the Pythagorean Theorem formula.	Whiteboard Markers
10 mins	Application and Examples	Present real-world problems and guide students in applying the discovered formula to solve them.	Projector Problem examples
15 mins	Independent Discovery	Students independently apply the theorem to solve additional problems. Circulate to assist and discuss.	Worksheets Calculators
10 mins	Assessment	Formative assessment through a quick problem-solving challenge or reflection.	Handouts Exit tickets
5 mins	Conclusion and Homework	Summarize discoveries and key points.	Homework assignments

Time	Activity	Description	Materials
		Assign homework: exploration and problem-solving tasks.	

Detailed Lesson Breakdown

1. Introduction (10 mins)

- **Objective:** Engage students and set the stage for discovery-based learning.
- **Activity:**
    - Explain that the class will be discovering how to find the relationship between the sides of a right triangle.
    - State the objective: "Today, you will explore and uncover how to solve right triangles using the Pythagorean Theorem."

2. Exploration Activity 1 (15 mins)

- **Objective:** Enable students to explore geometric relationships in right triangles.
- **Activity:**
    - Distribute graph paper, rulers, and protractors.
    - Have students draw several right triangles of different sizes.
    - Measure the lengths of the sides and squares of these lengths, guiding them to observe patterns.
    - Ask students to cut out the squares and physically compare the areas.

3. Exploration Activity 2 (20 mins)

- **Objective:** Use technology to visualize and reinforce discoveries about the Pythagorean Theorem.
- **Activity:**
    - Divide students into small groups.

- o Have them use interactive geometry software like GeoGebra to construct right triangles and observe the relationships between the squares of the side lengths.
- o Encourage students to test various triangles and hypothesize the theorem.

4. Guided Discovery (15 mins)

- **Objective:** Facilitate the derivation of the Pythagorean Theorem from student observations.
- **Activity:**
  - o Gather the class and ask groups to share their observations.
  - o Write these observations on the board and guide students to articulate the Pythagorean Theorem: $a^2+b^2=c^2$
  - o Validate and formalize their findings into the theorem.

5. Application and Examples (10 mins)

- **Objective:** Apply the discovered theorem to practical examples.
- **Activity:**
  - o Present real-world problems, such as calculating the diagonal of a rectangle or the shortest path across a field.
  - o Demonstrate solving these problems using the theorem.
  - o Encourage students to apply their discovery to these examples.

6. Independent Discovery (15 mins)

- **Objective:** Provide individual practice in applying the theorem.
- **Activity:**
  - o Distribute worksheets with a variety of right triangle problems.
  - o Allow students to solve them independently, using their newfound understanding of the theorem.
  - o Circulate to offer guidance and check for comprehension.

7. Assessment (10 mins)

- **Objective:** Assess students' understanding through a practical task.
- **Activity:**
    - Provide a short problem-solving challenge or ask for a written reflection on what they discovered and how they applied it.
    - Collect exit tickets or quick write-ups for review.

8. Conclusion and Homework (5 mins)

- **Objective:** Summarize and reinforce key discoveries.
- **Activity:**
    - Recap the day's discoveries and their importance in solving right triangles.
    - Assign homework that involves exploring real-world applications or additional problems using the Pythagorean Theorem.
    - Address any final questions or provide resources for further exploration.

Homework

- Complete the assigned exploration tasks and problem-solving exercises involving the Pythagorean Theorem from the textbook or worksheet. Write a brief explanation of how the theorem was discovered and applied.

Assessment Tools

- **Formative Assessment:** Observations during exploration activities, participation in discussions, and reflection responses.
- **Summative Assessment:** Accuracy of independent practice problems and quality of exit ticket responses.

Resources

- GeoGebra Interactive Geometry Tool
- Pythagorean Theorem Exploration Activities

Additional Notes

- Encourage students to think critically and share their insights during the discovery activities.
- Adapt exploration complexity based on student engagement and understanding.
- Consider using real-life applications relevant to students' interests for increased engagement.

APPENDIX F:SAMPLE FACULTY EVALUATION FORM

Full-Time Teaching Faculty Evaluation Worksheet

Instructor Name: _________________________________   Date: ___________

Dept./Program: _________________________________   Evaluation Period: ___________

Evaluator: _________________________________   Tenured: ☐Y ☐N

INSTRUCTIONS:
On the scales provided below, ranging from Unacceptable to Exceptional, indicate a rating for each Standard. All ratings must be justified. The rating levels for the extremities are Unacceptable (U) and Exceptional (E).

STANDARD 1: Syllabus Development & Presentation:
Faculty members do not need to fulfill all of the listed examples to be considered exceptional.

Examples of exceptional performance might include:
  a. Syllabus has all the applicable elements as indicated in CSN Syllabus Policy.
  b. Syllabus learning outcomes meet program accreditation needs, if applicable.
  c. Syllabus has a clear description of grading.
  d. Syllabus is clear, organized, relevant, easy to read, and free of grammatical errors & typos.
  e. Syllabus is consistent in appearance (font size, face, style, etc.).
  f. Faculty assesses student understanding of course policies, procedures and syllabus.
  g. Faculty makes syllabus and all relevant policies available in electronic format within the first week of classes.
  h. Faculty holds a question/answer session during the first week devoted to addressing all student's questions
  i. Faculty creates and uses an online forum to address concerns/questions about policies and procedures with students.

  j. Other, as agreed upon by the department/program: _________________________________

STANDARD 2: Course Materials and Curricula Development:
Faculty members do not need to fulfill all of the indicated examples to be considered exceptional.

Examples of exceptional performance might include:
a. Course materials are current and reflect knowledge of best practices in the field.
b. Course materials are developed and updated so that they correspond to the catalog description and student learning outcomes.
c. Course materials demonstrate a variety of teaching strategies.
d. Assessment tools measure the students' attainment of the course objectives.
e. Creates textbook and/or computerized materials for specific classes.
f. Develops new courses as requested.
g. Research and recommend the revision, deletion or addition of programs and courses to reflect the changes occurring within the subject area.
h. Participate in evaluation of curricula and instruction.
i. Participate in the evaluation of instructional takeout materials.
j. Evaluate and recommend catalog revisions.
k. Participate in program, department school and college accreditation activities.

l. Other, as agreed upon by the department/program: ____

STANDARD 3: Content Presentation:
Faculty members do not need to fulfill all of the indicated examples to be considered exceptional.

Examples of exceptional performance might include:
a. Presentation is well organized.
b. Uses multiple techniques to present material.
c. Uses ongoing summary and review techniques to ensure student understanding.
d. Pacing of material is appropriate to meet course objectives.
e. Utilizes current and up to date information and examples in instructional environment.
f. Incorporates technology into teaching.
g. Uses time efficiently and effectively.
h. Presents material as identified in the course description in accordance with the learning outcomes.
i. Effectively uses methods to project enthusiasm when interacting with students.
Demonstration of good English usage and, if applicable, oral presentation skills.

i. Other, as agreed upon by the department/program:

STANDARD 4: Student Engagement and Participation:
Faculty members do not need to fulfill all of the indicated examples to be considered exceptional.

Examples of exceptional performance might include:
a. Encourages class discussions, when appropriate.
b. Engages students with questions.
c. Uses both individual and group projects and presentations, if appropriate.
d. Creates an environment where students feel respected, valued and encouraged to share diverse viewpoints.
e. Learns students' names and encourages them to learn and use one another's names.
f. Responds appropriately to student's questions and challenges within the instructional environment.
g. Effectively demonstrates methods to assure frequent student-faculty professional contact in and out of classes.

h. Other, as agreed upon by the department/program: ____

APPENDIX F

STANDARD 5: Evaluation of Student Learning:
Faculty members do not need to fulfill all of the indicated examples to be considered exceptional.

Examples of exceptional performance might include:
   a. Graded assessments and other course work are returned to students with feedback and in a timely fashic
   b. Students are given suggestions for improvement.
   c. Keeps current and accurate records of student progress.
   d. Periodically provides students with feedback on their performance of the required course work.
   e. Students can always check their cumulative performance at any time during the course.
   f. Explains to students how to understand the provided information on their cumulative performance at any point in the course.
   g. Submits grades in conformity with college procedures and deadlines.

   h. Other, as agreed upon by the department/program: ____

STANDARD 6: Student Communication and Support:
Faculty members do not need to fulfill all of the indicated examples to be considered exceptional.

Examples of exceptional performance might include:
   a. Announce a minimum of five office hours a week and keep them routinely.
   b. Offers students help outside of office hours.
   c. Answers phone messages and emails within time limits announced in the course syllabus.
   d. Advise students on supplemental reading or experience opportunities for further understanding of the subject area.
   e. Advise students on career alternatives and opportunities related to the subject area.
   f. Advise students on the types of services and assistance that are available to students who are failing to make satisfactory progress toward meeting the course's objectives.
   g. Advise students on additional courses that might be taken by the student in the subject area or in related subject areas.
   h. Tutor students in related courses.

   i. Other, as agreed upon by the department/program: ____

STANDARD 7: Course Logistics, Proficiency and Professionalism:
Faculty members do not need to fulfill all of the indicated examples to be considered exceptional.

Examples of exceptional performance might include:
   a. Within the appropriate timeframe, submits textbook and technology requests.
   b. Requests for photocopies are timely and in accordance with CSN policies/procedures.
   c. Requests for library materials are timely.
   d. Researches and reviews new books/materials and works with publishers to upgrade books/materials.
   e. Maintains proficiency and, if necessary, required certifications in academic area.
   f. Improves course content knowledge.
   g. Invites colleagues to evaluate course materials and instruction, if appropriate.
   h. Evaluate colleagues' course materials and instruction.
   i. Attend and participate in School/Department/Program meetings.
   j. Cooperate with supervisors and the college administration to achieve the goals of the institution.
   k. Treat students, colleagues and staff with courtesy and respect.
   l. Comply with all sections of the NSHE code and policies concerning Professional Conduct applicable to faculty.

   m. Other, as agreed upon by the department/program: ____

ABOUT THE AUTHOR

Lisa Savy Kauffman brings over three decades of rich teaching experience to the field of education. Since her teaching career began in 1985, Lisa has dedicated 17 years to inspiring high school students across all levels of mathematics and computer programming. Her journey in education continued to flourish as she transitioned to teaching at the college level in 2011, where she has expertly guided students through a spectrum of courses ranging from College Algebra to Differential Equations.

Lisa's passion for integrating technology and mathematics led her to author the innovative textbook, ***Programming Precalculus with Python***, a work she believes will revolutionize the way precalculus is taught by merging traditional concepts with modern computational techniques.

Lisa's academic foundation is as impressive as her teaching portfolio. She earned her B.S. in Mathematics-Computer Science from UCLA, followed by an M.Ed from UCLA and an M.A. in Mathematics from UC Riverside. Her educational background, coupled with her extensive teaching experience, empowers her to bridge the gap between theory and practice, making complex mathematical concepts accessible and engaging for her students.

Lisa has given several presentations at Mathematics and Technology Conferences, including AMATYC (American Mathematical Association of Two-Year Colleges) and ICTCM (International Conference on Technology in Collegiate Mathematics).

In her ongoing commitment to educational excellence, Lisa continues to explore new methodologies and technologies to enhance learning outcomes and inspire the next generation of mathematicians and programmers.

www.ingramcontent.com/pod-product-compliance
Lightning Source LLC
Chambersburg PA
CBHW071329140726
47996CB00005B/1889